W9-ARN-448

GREAT NEWS FOR THE WORLD

By the same author

GOD'S TRUTH
A scientist shows why it makes sense to believe the Bible.

PLANET EARTH'S LAST HOPE
The Christian answer to the environmental crisis

GREAT NEWS
FOR
THE WORLD

Alan Hayward

CHRISTADELPHIANS WORLDWIDE

Christadelphians Worldwide
Dept. 153 B
3 Regent Street
Birmingham B1 3HG

Copyright © Alan Hayward 1976
First published 1976
Reprinted 1976

All rights reserved

0 9504436 0 3

Printed in Great Britain by
Hazell Watson and Viney Ltd,
Aylesbury, Bucks

CONTENTS

Acknowledgments 6

1. First the bad news 7

2. Rescue operation 13

3. Flight path for a nation 20

4. All change 29

5. Jailbreak 39

6. The dotted line 49

7. Into the unknown 59

8. Plan for a planet 67

9. An ancient faith in modern dress 81

10. Can we afford it? 90

Notes and references 93

Publishers' note 96

ACKNOWLEDGMENTS

The Scripture quotations in the book, except where otherwise stated, are from the Revised Standard Version of the Bible, copyrighted 1946 and 1952 by the Division of Christian Education of the National Council of the Churches of Christ in the USA.

A few quotations, indicated by the abbreviation TEV, are taken from Good News for Modern Man – The New Testament in Today's English Version, copyrighted 1966 by the American Bible Society, New York.

A few quotations, indicated by the abbreviation NEB, are from the New English Bible, Second Edition © 1970 by permission of Oxford and Cambridge University Presses.

Permission to use these is gratefully acknowledged.

Quotation from the King James (Authorised) Version are denoted by KJV, and those from the Revised Version by RV.

The globe on the cover is copyrighted © Rand McNally & Company, R.L. 75–Y–97.

1

FIRST THE BAD NEWS

Sometimes when I am playing with my three year old grand-daughter a lump comes into my throat, and I think of words spoken by Sir Winston Churchill some twenty years ago.

The British Government had just decided to go ahead with the manufacture of hydrogen bombs. Some members of parliament were opposed to this, and a debate took place in the House of Commons. Prime Minister Churchill made a speech defending his decision, in which he said to a hushed chamber:

'What ought we to do? Which way can we turn to save our lives and the future of the world?

'It does not matter so much to old people. They are going soon, anyway. But I find it poignant to look at youth in all its activity and ardour, and, most of all, to watch little children playing their merry games and wonder what would lie before them if God wearied of mankind.'[1]

Churchill was right. It is our little children who have the most to lose, and the prospect for their future is horrifying. The fearful weapons that he saw with his imagination are now reality. Britain, America, Russia, China, France, India and Israel, already belong to the World Suicide Club (membership open to all who possess atomic bombs) and other nations are queuing up to join.

But the position today is even worse than Churchill feared. An explosive situation is developing all over the world, because a horrifying new dimension has recently been added: famine. No sensible nation would ever start a nuclear war. But hunger sometimes drives people to do crazy things.

Shortages of Everything – Except People

It simply had to happen, sooner or later. During the past forty years the world's population has doubled. That means two thousand million extra mouths to feed.

There would have been a disastrous famine long before had it not been for one thing. During the same period the world output of food has roughly doubled, too.

But the world's farmers cannot keep on increasing their output like this. Their success over the past forty years has been due to several factors. New land has been brought under cultivation; dry areas have been made more productive by large-scale irrigation schemes; and the use of fertilisers and of agricultural machinery has been dramatically increased.

Unfortunately, none of these advances can be repeated. There is hardly any more good agricultural land lying unused, waiting to be brought under cultivation. Most of the earth's rivers have already been harnessed, so that there are already signs of a world shortage of water. Both fertilisers and fuel for farm machinery are scarce, and their prices have recently increased by several hundred per cent.

Farsighted farmers are becoming increasingly concerned. Modern agriculture is totally dependent on the products of modern technology. These, in turn, depend upon the world's supplies of mineral resources which are very limited.

Fertilisers cannot be made without phosphates. But we have been mining the world's phosphates for years and years without a thought for the future – and now we are beginning to run short. To build tractors you need metals like tin, zinc, platinum and copper – and now we are gradually running out of those metals. To run tractors you need oil – but the world's oil looks as if it will all be used up within a few tens of years.

It is not surprising that world food production has been more or less at a standstill for the past three years. This means that the amount of food that barely fed the world's 3,800 million people in 1973 must be stretched to feed 4,000 million in 1976. And next year there will be another 75 million wanting a share, and a further 76 million the year after, and yet another 78 million the year after that ...

Thanks to pollution, even pure air and pure seawater are becoming scarce. Dr. Jacques Cousteau, the world's leading expert in oceanography, told a conference in 1975, 'The oceans could be dead in less than 50 years.' Ominously, he added, 'Ecologists know very well that the human species cannot survive if the oceans die.' [2]

These are the basic facts behind the economic problems facing Britain and the USA and every other nation today. Prices were bound to rise, and are bound to go on rising. Prices always do rise in times of shortage, and the world is short of nearly everything – except people.

In the wealthier nations rising prices will lead to inflation or to increasing unemployment, or to a fall in our standard of living – or, quite probably, to all of these.

In the poorer countries of Asia and Africa and Latin America the effects will be far more disastrous. Hundreds of millions of their inhabitants are already spending almost their entire incomes on food. Rising prices can mean only one thing to them: starvation.

The Way We Are Going

No one can be sure what the next few years will bring. Only one thing is certain. Unless mankind can work out some sort of solution within the next few years we shall all be facing catastrophe.

Many westerners are puzzled by the population explosion. Why, they ask, don't the famine-stricken nations of the Third World curb their fantastic population growth?

There are three good reasons why they do not. In the first place, a population explosion is rather like a runaway train. There is no way to stop it suddenly, you can only slow it down gradually. Two-fifths of the population in countries like India are under 15 (compared with one-fifth in countries like Britain). This vast army of children will become parents themselves within a few years.

Secondly, trying to persuade people in the Third World to limit their families is as soul-destroying a job as selling raincoats in the Sahara. Poverty-stricken peasants depend on their children to support them in old age. Naturally, they are all determined to have as many children as possible.

Finally, many Afro-Asian governments resent even the suggestion that they should solve the world crisis by controlling their own populations. They fail to see why they should take drastic steps of this kind just so that the wealthiest one-third of the world can go on consuming two-thirds of the world's food and resources.

As they see it there is only one fair way of tackling the problem. They think there ought to be a drastic redistribution of the world's wealth; in other words, that we Europeans should deliberately reduce our living standards so that they can increase theirs.

This may seem a monstrous impertinence to us. But everything depends upon one's point of view. To the man in the rice paddy it sounds a perfectly reasonable suggestion. What he regards as an almost incredible piece of cheek is our suggestion that he should limit his desire for children, while we go on indulging our apparently limitless appetite for food and comfort!

So the vicious circle remains unbroken. The tropical nations cannot and will not reduce their enormous rate of population growth. The wealthy nations will not voluntarily reduce their extravagant use of the earth's limited resources. The situation calls for co-ordinated, unselfish

action by every nation and every individual; but there is
not the slightest hope that this will happen.

Countdown to Catastrophe

Meanwhile time is running out. Every time the clock ticks
the world's population is increased by two. Ten thousand
additional hungry mouths join us every hour.

There is no longer any question as to whether a major
world disaster is coming. The only questions are when
and what form it will take.

Will our economic system stand up to the increasing
strains being placed upon it? Can our democratic way of
life survive, or will social unrest and violence escalate into
revolution?

Will the population problem be solved eventually by
a hundred million people starving to death each year? Or
by the horrors of an all-out nuclear war?

Increasing numbers of influential sources are now giving gloomy answers to questions like these. In 1975 the
leading British newspaper, *The Observer*, began an article
which was afterwards reproduced as a widely circulated
booklet with these words:

'We and our children are approaching a world of
mounting confusion and horror. The next 25 years, possibly the next decade, will bring starvation to hundreds
of millions, and hardship, disorder or war to most of
the rest of us. Democracy, where it exists, has little
chance of survival. Nor in the longer run has our indus-
trial way of life. There will not be a "better tomorrow" beyond our present troubles.'[3]

Frightening though *The Observer*'s predictions may be,
other writers are even more pessimistic. Some are afraid
that the famous last prophecy of the futurist writer H. G.
Wells will soon be proved true:

'This world is at the end of its tether. The end of everything we call life is close at hand and cannot be evaded ... There is no way out or round or through the impasse. It is the end.'[4]

Happily, it can be said with absolute certainty that Wells was wrong in his conclusion. So are all the present-day prophets of doom.

This is not to say that they overestimate the dangers facing mankind. The situation is indeed desperate. The problems confronting our generation are quite beyond our ability to solve. An appalling disaster really is looming up ahead of us, and there is nothing that *we* can do to avert it.

But the doom-mongers generally overlook one vital fact. Two thousand years ago, when the human race was sunk in obscenity and wickedness, someone called Jesus of Nazareth came to the world's aid. He only taught for about four years, but he changed the whole course of human history. And he left behind him a promise that one day he would come to the world's rescue a second time, when all mankind was in dire need of his help.

This is not wishful thinking. As we shall see in the next chapter, it is plain, well-attested historical fact that he made this promise. And as Chapter 3 will show, there is a great deal of compelling evidence that his promise will be fulfilled – soon!

Truly, this is Great News for the World.

RESCUE OPERATION

Nevil Shute's best-seller, *No Highway*, is a novel about a scientist in the Royal Aircraft Establishment. Shute wanted to portray his hero as a weird eccentric. So he depicted him as a man who didn't know what a dishmop was for; and what's more, a man who actually believed in the second coming of Christ.

The reading public lapped it up. Of course, anybody – especially a scientist – who believes in the Second Coming must be *very* odd!

In fact the only odd thing is the attitude of the public. No one regards the kings and queens of England as odd, or the archbishops of Canterbury, either. Yet for centuries every new British monarch, right down to the present queen, Elizabeth II, has been crowned by an archbishop uttering the words:

'I give thee, O Sovereign Lord (Lady), this crown to wear, until he who reserves the right to wear it *shall return*.'

Queen Victoria Was Not Amused

At least one British ruler has taken those words very seriously. A year after Queen Victoria died, Dean Farrar spoke in Canterbury Cathedral about a conversation between himself and the late queen.[1]

'Oh, how I wish that the Lord would come during my lifetime!' she remarked.

'Why does your Majesty feel this very earnest desire?' asked the Dean.

The queen replied: 'Because I should so love to lay my crown at his feet.'

Queen Victoria was not alone in holding this belief. President Abraham Lincoln used to attend a meeting place in Washington where lectures were given about the return of Christ.[2] In our own day, Dr. Billy Graham has told how the late President Kennedy asked him to explain the Second Coming to him; the President already believed in it, but wanted to learn more about it.[3]

Scientist Sir Isaac Newton's religious writings contain many references to the Second Coming.[4] To him, Christ's return was evidently as real and as important for mankind as the law of universal gravitation that made Newton famous.

In the very early days of Christianity everybody in the church believed in the Second Coming. As the historian Gibbon puts it, 'Those who understood in their literal sense the discourses of Christ himself were obliged to expect the second and glorious coming of the Son of Man ...'[5]

In theory all the great churches have always believed in the Second Coming. They all subscribe to the very ancient statement of Christian belief known as 'The Apostles' Creed'. And the Creed, which millions of people recite every week, proclaims:

'I believe ... in Jesus Christ ... he ascended into heaven, and sitteth on the right hand of God the Father Almighty, *from thence he shall come* to judge the quick and the dead.'

What Jesus Said

As Gibbon pointed out in the passage quoted above, if you take the teaching of Jesus Christ seriously you can't help believing that he will return. He promised it so often.

Once when Jesus spoke of his second coming he referred to the following passage from the Old Testament:

'And there shall be a time of trouble, such as never has been since there was a nation till that time; but at that time your people shall be delivered.' (DANIEL 12: 1)

This frightening picture of a 'time of trouble such as never has been' strikes a chord. It sounds remarkably like a description of where our own civilisation is heading. Moreover, Jesus himself applied these words of Daniel to his second coming in the Gospel of Matthew, chapter 24.

Jesus once began a discussion with his disciples by prophesying that the great temple in Jerusalem would be destroyed. (And so it was, when the Romans sacked Jerusalem about forty years later.) Horrified, the disciples asked two questions in one:

'Tell us, (1) when will this be, and (2) what will be the sign of your coming and of the close of the age?' (verse 3.)

The Lord Jesus spent the rest of Matthew 24 answering those two questions. Part of his reply relates specifically to the first question, but most of it is concerned with the other question, which was about his second coming. A few verses seem to be an answer to both questions at once. Here are some of the things that he said about his return in this chapter, with a few comments in brackets.

'Take heed that no one leads you astray. For many will come in my name, saying, "I am the Christ", and they will lead many astray.' (verses 4,5.)

(This actually happened in the early days of Christianity. The early Christians had such a fervent belief in Christ's return that unscrupulous impostors tried to cash in on it.)

'You will hear of wars and rumours of wars; see that you are not alarmed; for this must take place, but the end is not yet. For nation will rise against nation, and kingdom against kingdom, and there will be famines and earthquakes in various places: all this is but the beginning of the sufferings.' (verses 6–8.)

(Notice how Jesus warned his followers to be patient. He knew that people would frequently make the mistake of expecting him too soon, and so he gave this warning that many unpleasant things had to happen first.)

'This gospel of the kingdom will be preached throughout the whole world, as a testimony to all nations; and then the end will come.' (verse 14.)

(We have had to wait until the twentieth century to see this prophecy fulfilled. But thanks to the work of the Bible societies, and to radio and television, the words of Scripture are being read or heard today in every country on earth, including those behind the Iron Curtain. So now, at last, we may expect that 'the end will come'.) [6]

'Then there will be great tribulation, such as has not been from the beginning of the world until now, no, and never will be. And if those days had not been shortened, no human being would be saved; but for the sake of the elect those days will be shortened.' [7] (verses 21,22.)

(Thus Jesus foretold, nineteen centuries ago, what thoughtful men and women are only just beginning to realise today: that nothing less than the Second Coming can save the human race from extinction in the coming holocaust.)

'Immediately after the tribulation of those days the sun will be darkened (so it will be literally 'earth's darkest hour', as well as figuratively!) . . . then will appear the sign of the Son of man in heaven, and then all the tribes of the earth will mourn, and *they will see the Son of man coming on the clouds of heaven with power and great glory.*' (verses 29,30.)

More Promises of Christ's Return

There are dozens of places in the four Gospels where Jesus referred to his return. Here are just three of them, one each from the other three Gospels:

> 'Take heed, watch; for you do not know when the time will come. It is like a man going on a journey, when he leaves home and puts his servants in charge, each with his work, and commands the doorkeeper to be on the watch. Watch therefore – for you do not know when the master of the house (Jesus) will come, in the evening, or at midnight, or at cockcrow, or in the morning – lest he come suddenly and find you asleep.'
>
> (MARK 13: 33–36.)

> Then the Son of man will appear, coming in a cloud with great power and glory.' (LUKE 21: 27, TEV.)

> 'Jesus answered him, "If I want him to live on until I come, what is that to you?" ' (JOHN 21: 23, TEV.)

After the Gospels comes a book called The Acts of the Apostles. Here also the promise of the Second Coming rings loud and clear. In the very first chapter we are told how Jesus went up into heaven. As his apostles watched him go, two angels appeared to them with this message:

> 'Men of Galilee, why do you stand looking into heaven? This Jesus, who was taken up from you into heaven, *will come* in the same way as you saw him go into heaven.' (ACTS 1: 11.)

The apostles were quick to learn. Only a couple of pages later we find them preaching that God was bound to 'send the Christ . . . whom heaven must receive until the time.' (ACTS 3: 20,21.)

In their letters, which make up most of the rest of the

New Testament, the apostles spoke of the Second Coming something like a hundred times. Here are three examples:

PAUL: 'The Lord himself will descend from heaven with a cry of command.' (1 THESSALONIANS 4: 16.)

PETER: 'Set your hope fully upon the grace that is coming to you at the revelation of Jesus Christ.'
(1 PETER 1: 13.)

JOHN: 'Abide in him, so that when he appears we may have confidence and not shrink from him in shame at his coming.' (1 JOHN 2: 28.)

The Book of Revelation

The last book of the Bible, the Book of Revelation, is in a class of its own. Its first verse tells us its purpose: 'To show to his (Christ's) servants what must soon take place.' In other words, it is a book of prophecy about the future – and especially about the Second Coming and the events leading up to it.

It starts talking about the Second Coming on its first page: 'Behold, he is coming with the clouds, and every eye will see him.' (REVELATION 1: 7.) And it goes on talking about it until one verse before the end of the book: 'He who testifies to these things (Jesus) says, "Surely I am coming soon." Amen. Come, Lord Jesus!' (REVELATION 22: 20.)

In between, the Book of Revelation tells us of many terrible and exciting events that were to take place before Christ's return to the earth. It also contains numerous passages describing the Second Coming itself. Here is one of them.

'Then the seventh angel blew his trumpet, and there were loud voices in heaven, saying, "The kingdom of the world has become the kingdom of our Lord and of

his Christ, and he shall reign for ever and ever." And
the twenty-four elders who sit on their thrones before
God fell on their faces and worshipped God, saying,

> "We give thanks to thee, Lord God Almighty, who
> art and who wast,
> that thou hast taken thy great power and begun to
> reign.
> The nations raged, but thy wrath came,
> and the time for the dead to be judged,
> for rewarding thy servants, the prophets and saints,
> and those who fear thy name, both small and great,
> and for destroying the destroyers of the earth." '

(REVELATION 11 : 15–18.)

This shows that the following things will happen when
Christ comes back to rule over the earth:

(1) The nations will rage.
(2) God's punishments will fall upon them.
(3) The dead will be raised to judgment.
(4) God's true servants will be rewarded.
(5) *Those people who are destroying the earth will
themselves be destroyed.*

Now you will know why I spoke so confidently at the
end of Chapter 1. H. G. Wells was hopelessly mistaken.
Life on earth will not be wiped out, after all. God Himself
says so.

His Son will return when the world needs him desperately. He will be just in time to destroy those men who, if
left to themselves, really would destroy the earth.

3

FLIGHT PATH FOR A NATION

Today, more than ever before, the human race needs God's help. But how can we be sure there is a God? And even if He does exist, what proof is there that He has any active interest in our world?

These questions demand an answer. Before trying to provide one, let me tell you about the time I was invited into the flight deck of a big jet flying across Africa. The captain made me very welcome – almost too welcome for comfort, in fact. Turning his back on the flying controls he chatted away as if he hadn't a care in the world.

'Don't worry,' he smiled reassuringly. 'The automatic pilot is in full control. That will do my job for me for the next hour or so better than I could do it myself.'

Since I knew a bit about these electronic gadgets I had no reason to question him. But suppose that I had been doubtful, and had asked, 'How do I know there is such a thing? Can you show it to me?'

He might well have answered something like this. 'Sorry, I can't. It's too thoroughly boxed in. And even if I could, you wouldn't know what you were looking at. But I can prove to you that it's there, all right – and that it's working perfectly.'

'How?'

'By telling you what the flight path is, so that you can check it for yourself. In about a quarter of an hour you will see a great stretch of water dead ahead. That's the lake behind the Volta Dam. We fly right over the water, and in thirty-two minutes from now we shall cross the dam. Thirteen minutes later you'll see the Atlantic coastline in the distance. When that happens we shall be nearly at Accra

Airport. I'll take over the controls myself, then.'

There is a parallel to this in the way that God has been dealing with man. More than 3,000 years ago He began to reveal the 'flight path' that He had mapped out for the world.

He did not disclose the whole future history of every nation on earth. That would have been unnecessarily complicated. All that He needed to do was to map out the entire future history of one key nation, the Jews. He began like this, in about 1300 BC:

'If you will not obey the voice of the Lord your God or be careful to do all his commandments and his statutes which I command you this day, then all these curses shall come upon you . . . You shall be plucked off the land which you are entering to take possession of it.

'And the Lord will scatter you among all peoples, from one end of the earth to the other . . . And among these nations you shall find no ease, and there shall be no rest for the sole of your foot; but the Lord will give you there a trembling heart, and failing eyes, and a languishing soul; your life shall hang in doubt before you; night and day you shall be in dread, and have no assurance of your life. . . .

'And you shall become a horror, a proverb, and a by-word, among all the peoples where the Lord will lead you away.' (DEUTERONOMY 28: 15,63–66,37.)

According to Plan

All this happened exactly according to plan. The Assyrians and the Babylonians began to carry off the Jews into exile, six or seven centuries before Christ. The Romans finished the job during the first two centuries AD. From then until modern times the Jews were an extraordinary, unique people: the only nation on earth without a homeland.

Just as the prophecy quoted above (and numerous

others) foretold, the life of the Jews in their exile was made wretched by persecution. In the twentieth century Adolf Hitler tried to get rid of the Jews. But he was only the last, and the most ambitious, of a long line of Jew-murderers.

All through the Christian era there has never been a century when the Jews were not being persecuted or massacred somewhere. They have always been on the move. Sometimes this was because they were being forcibly deported, and sometimes because they were fleeing for their lives. And always they were despised, envied, suspected, hated.

This was the path that the Old Testament mapped out for them. This was the path they actually trod for twenty centuries or so. Can we reasonably doubt that some Unseen Pilot has been in control?

With so many people trying to exterminate the Jews, you might have thought they would have disappeared long ago. But no, God's 'flight path' laid it down very clearly that *the Jews would outlive all their persecutors.* These words were written some 2,500 years ago:

'Fear not, O Jacob my servant, says the Lord (Jacob was the other name of Israel, who gave his name to the Jewish nation, his descendants) for I am with you. *I will make a full end of all the nations to which I have driven you, but of you I will not make a full end.* I will chasten you in just measure, and I will by no means leave you unpunished.' (JEREMIAH 46: 28.)

When this prophecy was uttered it must have sounded wildly improbable. It was almost as if an aircraft captain were to announce:

'Ladies and gentlemen, I am sorry to tell you that we are in for a dangerous and unpleasant journey. There are hijackers on board who will do us quite a lot of harm.

'Also, we shall be flying through a most appalling storm. Bigger and stronger planes than ours are going to be forced down. But don't be too alarmed. We shall keep on flying, and we shall arrive eventually at our proper destination.'

Home – But Only Just

Admittedly, it says nothing about the Jewish nation reaching a destination in the verse quoted above. But in the previous verse it does. This reads as follows:

'Fear not, O Jacob my servant,
nor be dismayed, O Israel;
for lo, I will save you from afar,
and your offspring from the land of their captivity.
Jacob shall return and have quiet and ease,
and none shall make him afraid.'   (JEREMIAH 46 : 27.)

This prophecy needs to be split in two. The first half – down to, and including, the words in italics – has already been fulfilled.

Twentieth-century Jewish history, like all the rest of Jewish history, has been quite astonishing. The prickly little state of Israel, with its population of less than three million Jews, is one of the most influential nations on earth. Yet thirty years ago it did not exist.

In 1897 the land of Israel was known as Palestine. It was a province of the Turkish Empire, and its inhabitants were mostly Arabs. That year a group of wealthy Jews in Europe and America launched a new movement called Zionism for buying land in Palestine and settling European Jews upon it.

The scheme was an immediate success. By 1914 there were already 100,000 Jewish residents in Palestine. Then the Turkish government became unfriendly, and many of the Palestinian Jews had to leave in a hurry.

In 1917 the tide turned again when the British army defeated the Turks and occupied Palestine. To secure Jewish support in World War I, Britain then authorised Lord Balfour to promise Palestine to the Jews as a 'national home'. (Diplomacy being the devious business that it is, Britain also promised Palestine to the Arabs at about the same time, through Lawrence of Arabia. The Arabs have never forgiven Britain for playing this double game.)

Between the two wars Jewish immigration continued steadily. Hitler's persecution gave it a tremendous boost, until in 1948, when Britain pulled out, there were 650,000 Jews in the land.

They declared themselves to be 'The State of Israel', and fought for their very existence. To the world's astonishment they won. The new nation of Israel was born and has since survived attack after attack, despite the fierce opposition of Arab nations with more than a hundred times Israel's population.

Thus Jeremiah's prophecy that 'Jacob shall return' was fulfilled, incredibly, despite overwhelming odds. Clearly, the Unseen Pilot was still in control.

The Final Scene

The last part of the prophecy from Jeremiah quoted above shows no sign of being fulfilled yet. To the average Israeli, 'Jacob shall return and have quiet and ease and none shall make him afraid', sounds like a sick joke.

But this is only because the average Israeli does not understand his Old Testament. Take the following passage by the prophet Ezekiel:

'When the house of Israel dwelt in their own land, they defiled it by their ways and their doings . . . So I poured out my wrath upon them . . . I scattered them among the nations, and they were dispersed through the countries . . . But when they came to the nations, *wherever they came, they profaned my holy name* . . .

'Therefore say to the house of Israel, Thus says the

Lord God: *It is not for your sake, O house of Israel, that I am about to act,* but for the sake of my holy name, which you have profaned . . . For I will take you from the nations, and will gather you from all the countries, and bring you into your own land.

'I will sprinkle clean water upon you, and you shall be clean from all your uncleannesses, and from all your idols I will cleanse you. *A new heart I will give you,* and a new spirit I will put within you, and I will take out of your flesh the heart of stone.' (EZEKIEL 36: 17–26.)

There is a great deal to be learnt from those three paragraphs.

The first paragraph foretold that the Jews would be just as ungodly in their exile as they were before. This has undoubtedly come true.

Do not make the mistake of regarding Israel as an exceptionally wicked race. Every nation on earth falls a hundred miles short of God's high standards. The point is that Israel, the People of the Bible, were supposed to set the rest of the world an example. But they haven't. They are as bad as the rest of us.

The second paragraph reveals that God would bring the Jews back to their homeland despite their ungodliness, and not because they deserved any favours from Him.

This also has come true. Most Israelis are thoroughgoing materialists – just like most Europeans and Americans. Many of them are irreligious, and quite a lot are atheists. Of course they have not yet found the promised 'quiet and ease' – they are not yet fit for it.

The third paragraph explains what has still to happen. Only a miracle could transform the Jewish and Israeli peoples. Yet that miracle will take place. God has promised it: 'A new heart I will give you.'

This amazing change will occur when Israel's great Divine King ('Messiah', as they call him) appears. As another prophet says:

'I (God) will raise up for David a righteous Branch, and he shall reign as king and deal wisely, and shall execute justice and righteousness in the land. *In his days Judah will be saved and Israel will dwell securely*. And this is the name by which he will be called: "The Lord is our righteousness." ' (JEREMIAH 23: 5,6.)

Where Jesus Comes Into Jewish History

Here are just a few of the things the Old Testament prophesied about the Jewish Messiah:

(1) The Jews would reject him and kill him. (ISAIAH 53: 1–9; DANIEL 9: 26.)
(2) He would rise from the dead. (PSALM 16: 9–11; ISAIAH 53: 10,11.)
(3) He would ascend to heaven, dwell with God for a time, and eventually return to earth as king. (PSALM 110: 1,2; ISAIAH 53: 12.)

All these prophecies, except, of course, the last part of No. (3), were fulfilled by Jesus of Nazareth. So were many other Old Testament prophecies about Messiah, but unfortunately there is no time to consider those now.

The evidence of this great collection of fulfilled prophecies is conclusive. Jesus really is the Messiah, and will soon return to earth as King of the Jews. *Their* return to the land of Israel is a wonderful sign that *his* return is also near.

This agrees with the Lord Jesus Christ's own teaching. He spoke of the coming exile of the Jews like this:

'They will fall by the edge of the sword, and be led captive among all nations; and Jerusalem will be trodden down by the Gentiles (non-Jews), *until* the times of the Gentiles are fulfilled.' (LUKE 21: 24.)

Note that word 'until'. This is Jesus' way of saying,

'Watch the Jews. Watch the land of Israel. Watch Jerusalem! When it becomes a Jewish city again (which it did in 1967) you will know that world history is approaching its tremendous climax.'

Jesus immediately went on to say:

'Portents will appear in sun, moon, and stars.[1] On earth *nations will stand helpless, not knowing which way to turn* from the roar and surge of the sea; *men will faint with terror at the thought of all that is coming upon the world;* for the celestial powers will be shaken.[2] And then they will see the Son of man coming on a cloud with great power and glory.' (LUKE 21: 25–27, NEB.)

Look closely at the phrases printed in italics, bearing in mind that 'the surging sea' is a Bible metaphor for great hordes of men raging in fury. (see ISAIAH 17: 12,13.) The whole passage is a remarkable picture of the state our world looks like reaching within a few years.

Thus Jesus not only linked the return of the Jews with his second coming. He also revealed that his return would be to a world at its last gasp.

Prepare for Landing

Come back for a few moments to that airliner over Africa. We have flown the length of the Volta lake and passed right over its great dam, exactly as the captain had said we should.

There is no longer any room for doubt. Beyond all question, there must have been an automatic pilot keeping the plane on its prescribed course.

Now, exactly at the right time, we have just had our first glimpse of the Atlantic coast. Eagerly we return to our seats and fasten our belts. We know what that landmark means. Any minute now we shall start our descent for landing.

Mankind's journey through time is rather like that. Can we really doubt that there is an unseen God piloting our harassed world to a safe landing? He told us the flight path that He had mapped out for one special nation, and they have followed that path with astounding precision.

Now, at exactly the right time, just as our crisis-ridden civilisation is sinking towards catastrophe, we have seen the final landmark. After nearly 2,000 years the land of Israel has become a Jewish homeland again, and Jerusalem a Jewish city.

We know what that means. Any time now, Jesus Christ will be coming in to land.

Hadn't we better get out of our armchairs and prepare to meet him?

4

ALL CHANGE

The last time our friend Evelyn[1] came to see us she brought along her pet rat Cleopatra.

My wife and I, like most other people, have always felt a revulsion for rats. Previously, we could never understand how anybody could grow fond of a rodent. Within half an hour Cleopatra changed our attitude. But then Cleopatra is no ordinary rat.

To begin with she is beautifully clean, well groomed and fully house-trained. Her standards of personal hygiene would put any dog to shame, and many cats, too. Evelyn has given her a thorough examination in the pathology lab at her college, which Cleopatra passed with flying colours. She was found to be carrying far fewer germs than the average healthy human.

Cleopatra is surprisingly affectionate. When she snuggles under her mistress' chin, or rolls over so that her tummy can be tickled, she looks a picture of contentment. Watching her, you feel that here is a creature who has reached the summit of ratty happiness.

She has come a long way from her cousins living a paw-to-mouth existence in garbage dumps and sewers, riddled with vermin and disease, and in daily peril from traps and poison, dogs and cats. But if you were able to communicate with a wild rat and offer to turn him into a pet like Cleopatra, he would probably laugh at the suggestion.

'What, give up my way of life and take on a new one? No fear! I don't want to be washed and disinfected and trained and bossed about by some human. I'm all right as I am. I'm free to do just what I like, and I want to stay that way, thank you. Freedom – that's the life for me!'

Prisoners All

We must not press the parallel too far, because human beings are not rats and in many important ways are very different indeed. Yet the fact remains that many people do have an attitude very like that of the indignant rat.

They talk about freedom as if they possessed it. But they don't. None of us do, not even in the most liberal democracy on earth. Like the sewer rat, we are all prisoners of our environment.

If I am blinded in a car crash, or if a terrorist bomb blows my legs off, there is nothing I can do about it. I should have no choice but to go through life horribly disabled. If I contract leukaemia when I am young, or my heart fails when I am old, then I am not free to do anything but die.

If I see the world drifting towards a nuclear holocaust I am free to weep at the prospect of an end to civilisation. But I am powerless to prevent it. Even if I were a prime minister or a president I should still be a prisoner of circumstances. Freedom, real freedom, just does not exist in this complex world of ours.

Above all, we are the prisoners of our own temperaments. Everybody knows what Paul meant when he wrote:

'Though the desire to do good is in me, I am not able to do it. I don't do the good I want to do; instead, I do the evil that I do not want to do . . . What an unhappy man I am!' (ROMANS 7: 18–24, TEV.)

It is not only religious people who sometimes feel like that. Agnostics and atheists are aware of the same sort of conflict within them. The ability to think in terms of 'right' and 'wrong' is one of the qualities that distinguishes man from the animals.

Fair Play

This possession of a moral faculty is one of the most remarkable things about human nature. But even more extraordinary is the way that nearly every human being on earth seems to feel quite strongly about what is usually called 'fair play'.

A sense of fair play is not the same thing as a sense of right and wrong, although, of course, the two are related. Different civilisations have always had very different ideas as to what constitutes right and wrong. So have different individuals within any group. But there has always been an astonishing measure of agreement among mankind as to what constitutes fair play.

For instance, people differ as to whether a man should have one wife, or several. People differ as to whether it is permissible for a married man to have affairs with other women. But everybody, everywhere, agrees that the man who leaves his middle-aged invalid wife to starve, while he runs off to the Bahamas with a wealthy young widow, is a rotter.

Similarly, people argue as to whether it is right to drop bombs on enemy cities in wartime, knowing that lots of innocent women and children will be killed. But everybody, everywhere, agrees that the soldier who betrays his own comrades in the middle of the war, just because he sees his own side losing and wants to move over to the winning side, is worse than vermin.

Then again, opinions may differ as to whether the legendary Robin Hood was justified when he robbed the rich to feed the poor. But everybody, everywhere, despises the rich man who steals the pennies from a blind beggar's tray.

These three examples all point to the same conclusion: *a dirty trick is a dirty trick, all the world over* – and, so far as history can tell us, it always has been so.

Perhaps this seems to you such an obvious fact that you

wonder, why make so much fuss about it. There is, in fact, a very good reason for stressing this point.

We live in a world where Christianity has been on the defensive for a hundred years or more. Atheist philosophy has made it difficult for millions of people to believe in God. The importance of the fact outlined above – this stubborn, inescapable fact that practically all men, everywhere, despise dirty tricks – is that it cuts atheism down to size.

The main plank in the atheist platform is the belief that the theory of evolution explains all the mysteries of life. There is no space here to discuss whether evolution is a satisfactory explanation for the existence of the lower forms of life.[2] All I can hope to do now is to show that man cannot possibly have evolved from the animals, because evolution would have been bound to produce a race of men that admired dirty tricks and despised fair play!

'Survival of the Dirtiest'

The basis of the theory that man evolved from lower animals is the principle of natural selection, or, as it is often called, 'the survival of the fittest'.

In very simple terms natural selection is thought to operate like this. Every so often some chance reshuffling of molecules (technically known as a 'mutation') occurs. This causes an animal to be born with some advantage over its fellows. For instance, a lion might appear with a heavier jawbone and stronger jaw-muscles than the other lions.

In normal times this well endowed animal gets more to eat than his neighbours. In time of famine he really comes into his own. Then the strong-jawed lion grabs the only available piece of meat from his weaker, hungry brother. The well-fed lion gorges himself and lives to reproduce his kind, while the hungry one starves to death.

A dirty trick? Of course! That is how natural selection is supposed to work. The survival of the fittest really means, so far as the higher animals are concerned, the survival of the dirtiest and the trickiest.

How, then, did man come by his love of fair play and his hatred of dirty tricks? If atheist philosophy is correct, our ancestors survived because they *excelled* at dirty tricks. Yet we have acquired a deep distaste for dirty tricks – a revulsion against the very process that is supposed to have formed us! Clearly, the atheist has a tremendous problem on his hands.

Taking the argument a stage further, how is it that a great many men and women have a respect for unselfishness, kindness, compassion and conscientiousness? They may not practise these virtues very often themselves, but at least they admire them in others.

Yet these high moral ideals are a positive handicap in the struggle for survival. If the atheists' explanation of our origin is correct, then these virtues should have died out long ago, along with our love of fair play. Like the strong lion, the iron-hard men whose watchword was, 'Might is right, and I don't give tuppence for anybody else', should have been the only ones to survive.

Their brash, self-centred descendants should now be occupying the whole earth, if – IF – the atheists were right.

As it is, mankind's widespread respect for what has been called 'The Law of Decent Behaviour'[3] shows that man must have been created by some great Lawgiver.

The Explanation that Fits

There is an account of man's origin in the early chapters of the Bible that makes remarkably good sense. Though there are problems in reconciling Genesis with science it can be done,[4] and the outcome is an explanation that really does fit all the facts.

It begins in Genesis 1, which tells us that the first man was created in God's own image. (verses 26,27.) This immediately sets the human race apart from the rest of creation. Man alone can commune with God, understand what

God requires of him, and consciously obey God – or disobey God, if he chooses. Man alone was created in a very close relationship with his Creator – 'Adam the son of God', he was called. (LUKE 3: 38.) ... No wonder man has a sense of fair play!

Then God put this first man, Adam, to a simple test. God said:

> 'You may freely eat of every tree of the garden; but of the tree of knowledge of good and evil you shall not eat, for in the day that you eat of it you shall die.'
>
> (GENESIS 2: 16,17.)

We do not know what would have happened if the first man had obeyed God. The fact is that he did not. Genesis 3 tells us that our ancestors sinned, were sentenced to death, and were expelled from God's presence.

These events are presented to us as historical facts. Jesus Christ evidently accepted them as actual history, and I have never seen any convincing reasons why we should not do so, too – even though we do not know their date or their geographical location.

This record in Genesis is extremely important because it teaches a lesson affecting all human life, including our lives today. What happened to Adam and Eve happens, in one way or another, to every one of us also. As the New Testament explains:

> 'Sin came into the world through one man and death through sin, and so death spread to all men because all men sinned.' (ROMANS 5: 12.)

Children of Adam

So the whole human race is in the same unhappy position as Adam. He started off on the wrong foot, and the whole of mankind has been on the wrong road ever since. He went astray, and received his double punishment: im-

mediate banishment from God, and the certain knowledge that one day he would die.

No doubt Adam went out from the presence of God
sorrowfully, his mind filled with memories and with
thoughts of what might have been. He never for one
moment would have imagined he was gaining his freedom. He knew he was losing it.

Eden, the place where God walked, was the place of
freedom. To him, the rest of this wonderful world had
become one great prison, a place to live in sorrow until at
last God's sentence of death took effect.

It is tragic that so many people nowadays are unaware
of their real position. They cannot see that they are in just
the same situation as poor Adam – sinful, condemned by
God, and thrust out from His presence.

Yet there is powerful evidence that this is so. We still
bear within us the signs of both our lofty origin and our
tragic fall. Our deep-seated love of 'fair play' is the evidence that we really were once created in the image of
God. And the way we keep tripping up, failing to 'play
fair' despite our good intentions, is proof that we belong
to a blighted, sinful race.

These facts about the origin of mankind explain why so
many of us go through life dissatisfied. It is as if we are
always searching frantically for something that eludes us.

Materially, men and women in the western world are
better off than ordinary people have ever been before. But
they are still discontented. The real prizes, peace of mind
and lasting happiness, are always just out of reach.

This is because we have forgotten what we are searching
for. We know that something is amiss, but we don't know
what it is. We have lost sight of the fact that the world is
really a prison, and that we are the prisoners serving out
our sentences.

Finding Freedom

When I saw clean, affectionate, contented, happy Cleopatra I felt sorry for the wild rats of the sewers. But there was nothing I could do about it. The sewer rats do not know what they are missing, and have no wish to change. It is beyond human power to turn any of them into another Cleopatra.

God must feel something like that when He looks at the human race. He would like to lift us out of our prison, clean us up, change our habits, train us, and one day give us the perfect happiness that we yearn for.

That is just what Jesus offered people – real freedom:

'If you continue in my word, you are truly my disciples, and you will know the truth, and *the truth will make you free.*' (JOHN 8: 31,32.)

His listeners bristled. Like the wild rats, they considered they were free already. 'We ... have never been in bondage to anyone!' they slammed back at him. (JOHN 8: 33.)

Even the Son of God could do nothing with such people. He continued for a while trying to shatter their complacency, but it was of no avail. Before long they were threatening him with violence. (JOHN 8: 59.)

As Jesus told them, the truth could have made them free. But the truth about themselves was painful. (It nearly always is.) They chose to live in cloud-cuckoo-land and pretend there was nothing wrong with them.

So do most of us, most of the time. But unless we can somehow break free of that habit, we shall let slip the most precious thing in the world.

Everlasting Happiness

Everlasting life is a subject that is very much misunderstood. Sometimes people think of it as little more than a continuation of our present tear-stained existence. This often leads them to conclude that perhaps eternal life is not really worth having, after all.

Others look upon it as a sort of king-sized Christmas

present that God will hand out, one day, to the people who please Him. And since God is good and kind, they often conclude that He will probably give that gift to everybody – or, at any rate, nearly everybody.

Both these ideas are terribly wrong. Everlasting life is best thought of as everlasting happiness, or everlasting joy, which is how the Bible describes it. (ISAIAH 35 : 10.) The Bible also tells us that this happiness will be enjoyed in the presence of God. (REVELATION 21 : 3,4.)

Now you can only find great happiness in someone's company if you have grown to love that person. Cleopatra's idea of bliss is to be cuddled and tickled by her mistress. But a sewer rat would run a mile rather than submit to human caresses.

In the very nature of things, then, everlasting happiness can be enjoyed only by those who have, so to speak, grown to enjoy God's company. We can only do that by letting Him teach us how to enjoy being with Him. And that means letting Him do a tremendous job with us.

To begin with, we must recognise that this world of ours really is a prison, and a very foul one at that, and that because of our disobedience the sentence upon us is just. We must allow Him to lift us out of the filth, wash us, and set us going along a very different path. We must let Him turn the rest of our life into a training course, gradually developing in us the sort of character that really would enjoy living for ever in His presence.

Total Surrender

God is a perfectionist. He insists upon giving us a complete cure, and nothing less. And that calls for total surrender on our part. As the Bible puts it:

'I implore you by God's mercy *to offer your very selves* to him; a living sacrifice, dedicated and fit for his acceptance . . . Adapt yourselves no longer to the pattern of this present world, but *let your minds be remade and your whole nature thus transformed.'* (ROMANS 12 : 1,2, NEB.)

Those who decide to surrender their lives to God like this are often surprised. It is not the painful process that many of them expected it to be. In many ways it is a delight. But then the Lord Jesus Christ promised that it would be:

'Take my yoke upon you, and learn from me; for I am gentle and lowly in heart, and you will find rest for your souls. For my yoke is easy, and my burden is light.' (MATTHEW 11 : 29,30.)

Despite this, only a very small minority of mankind has ever been willing to submit. Jesus knew that this would be so:

'The gate is wide and the way is easy, that leads to destruction, and those who enter by it are many. For the gate is narrow and the way is hard, that leads to life, and those who find it are few.' (MATTHEW 7 : 13,14.)

At first sight those are discouraging words. A narrow gate – a hard way – few people finding everlasting life – why, this is indeed a daunting prospect!

Don't despair. This is only one half of a complex picture. Look back a few lines to the previous quotation, and see how the Lord also said that his yoke is easy, and his burden light. In the next two chapters we shall begin to see how the two halves of the picture fit together.

5

JAILBREAK

Commander Henry Macdonald was a naval officer of the old school. Transparently honest, he would no more think of telling a lie than of running his ship aground.

'I go to church because I believe in Christian morality,' he once said to me. 'But I don't claim to be a Christian. The very heart of the Christian religion doesn't make sense to me.'

'Why?' I asked.

'This business of the cross of Christ. How can any intelligent man believe in a God of love, and at the same time say that God needed a human sacrifice to appease His wrath? It just doesn't add up.'

Macdonald's problem is shared by millions. This is curious, because there is really no problem at all. The difficulty is due to a complete misunderstanding.

Jesus did not die to appease an angry God. His sacrifice was the most important event in history, and vitally necessary. But the real reason for it, as given in the Bible, has become distorted in many people's minds.

We have seen how human beings are really prisoners, of circumstances and of their own weak human nature. If only we can break out of that prison we can rise to undreamed-of heights of fulfilment and happiness. Outside our prison there is God, and only in God's presence can we find our joyful destiny.

The snag is that the prison has us completely in its grip. Our trouble is not so much that the walls are impregnable, as that we have lost all desire to escape. We are set in our ways, we even try to pretend that the prison is really a very fine place, or that we are not really in prison at all.

The power of the prison lies in our own apathy and weakness. That is why it is an almost impossible task to get us out. Jesus came – and died – to achieve that near-impossibility. His mission was:

> 'To open the eyes that are blind,
> To bring out the prisoners from the dungeon,
> From the prison those who sit in darkness.'
>
> (ISAIAH 42:7.)

The Man From Outside

The first problem was to wake up the prisoners. They had to be made aware that they really were in prison, that it was a poor place to be in, and that it was worth making every effort to escape to the better world outside.

This meant that somebody representing 'outside' needed to appear within the prison walls, and let the prisoners know what they were missing. There was only one really convincing way for him to do this. He would have to live an 'outside' sort of life inside the prison. Then the prisoners would see for themselves that what he told them about life outside was true.

God could, of course, have sent an angel from heaven to live in this world and show us what heavenly life is like. But that would not have been very satisfactory. Men would not have been greatly impressed by the godly behaviour of an angel.

'That's all very well for him,' would have been the natural human reaction. 'But he doesn't know what it's like to be human. Angels don't understand our feelings. They don't suffer temptation like us. What's the use of showing us how angels behave? We are not angels, and never can be!'

What God actually did was much more appropriate. He arranged for someone very special to be born inside the prison, but who was capable of living like someone from 'outside'.

This was why the Lord Jesus Christ's mother was a virgin. The virgin birth was not the pointless, unnecessary miracle that some people imagine. It was an absolutely vital part of God's scheme.

To make the necessary impact Jesus had to be an 'insider', one of us. He had to be born within the prison of human nature. Physically, he had to be a man, subject to all the weaknesses, the frustrations and temptations that we have to endure. That is why his mother had to be an ordinary woman.

But Jesus could never have shown us what the 'outside' life was like if he had been an ordinary man, with two human parents. So God worked a great miracle on the young virgin, Mary. He caused her to conceive a child that was, in the full sense of the term, God's own Son.

In this way, so the Bible tells us, the Son of God was born. It is a great pity that some religious teachers think they can improve on the simple language of the Bible. With the best of intentions, but very unwisely, they choose to call the birth of Jesus an 'incarnation'. They are not content with the Biblical description of Jesus, Son of God, but prefer to think of him as God Almighty *in person*.

Far from helping our understanding, this only creates difficulties. Tanker-loads of ink have been used in attempts to explain how Jesus could be, at one and the same time, both God Himself and God's Son. But this is like trying to draw a square circle. It can't be done.

Perfection in Human Form

It is far better not to worry about these man-made theological tangles, and to stick to the simple facts of the Bible narrative.

Through his mother, Jesus was every inch a man. Speaking literally, he was a member of our race, born inside the same prison.

Speaking figuratively, though, he was a 'man from outside', for two reasons. Because of his miraculous birth, he had what you might call a heavenly origin (even though, in the literal sense, he did not personally descend from heaven as an angel would have had to do).

In addition, Jesus really did live a life of heavenly quality, here on earth. Jesus is described as, 'the exact likeness of God's own being'. (HEBREWS 1 : 3, TEV.) Evidently he behaved just as God would have done, if God had come down to earth Himself. So Jesus was able to tell his disciples, 'He who has seen me has seen the Father.' (JOHN 14 : 8.)

This may sound an extravagant claim. If so, don't dismiss it too hastily. You will find it well worth while to read all four Gospels carefully before making up your mind about this.

You will find that the Gospels do not read like fiction. Somehow they have the ring of truth about them. The Jesus of the Gospels is not the sort of character that first-century writers could possibly have invented. Many a thoughtful unbeliever has reached the same conclusion after studying the Gospels: they read like true history.

And the central character of these extraordinary narratives is no ordinary man. Many of his words and deeds were misunderstood; shallow-minded men quickly wrote him off as unimportant. But those who took the trouble to understand him were overwhelmed.

'You are the Christ, the Son of the living God,' was their verdict. (MATTHEW 16 : 16.)

Those of us who have tried to get to know him today are similarly impressed. The more we study the Gospels, the more we realise that here was the ideal man. The life of Jesus is human life as it was meant to be lived, the kind of life for which we were really created.

His sort of life is the life that brings an infinite sense of fulfilment. No matter how hard we try, we cannot live up to his standards. But the closer we come to his example, the closer we are to finding peace, love and happiness.

His life certainly achieved its purpose. It showed very clearly that life inside the prison of our fallen nature is only a travesty, a poor shadow of the glorious life outside. Every man and woman who carefully looks at Jesus is likely to develop the same intense conviction. They will probably conclude:

'This prison is a far worse place than I realised. The free world outside is better than my wildest dreams. I want to become like Jesus. I want to be free!'

The Great Victory

Historians often enthuse about the world's most decisive battles, like Thermopylae, Waterloo and the Battle of Britain, when the whole course of human history balanced on a knife edge.

But they generally overlook the most important battle of all. Compared with this one the battles on their list were mere playground scuffles.

This battle was so decisive that the destiny of the whole human race revolved around it. Yet it was fought within the mind and the body of one man, Jesus the Son of God.

In him the strength of God and the weakness of human nature met, and were locked in mortal combat for a few suspense-packed years. Like Waterloo, it was a close-run battle of giants. Human nature was not defeated until the body of Jesus hung lifeless from the cross.

We see the battle approaching its climax a few hours before Jesus was crucified. There was still one last opportunity for him to run away. Should he take it? Or should he think only of his followers, and for their sake go forward to a horrible death?

'He withdrew from them about a stone's throw, and knelt down and prayed, "Father, if thou art willing, remove this cup from me; nevertheless not my will but thine, be done."

'And there appeared to him an angel from heaven, strengthening him. And being in an agony he prayed more earnestly: and his sweat became like great drops of blood falling down upon the ground.' (LUKE 22: 41–44.)

Shortly after, his enemies approached through the darkness of the garden. His decision made, he went forward to meet them and gave himself up. It was for a very good reason that he had chosen the horrors of crucifixion.

The hideous torture that he suffered was not in vain. It was his way – and God's way – of bursting open our prison wall.

Three Reasons for the Cross

Many things were accomplished by his willing death. There is space here to mention only three of them.

In the first place, his battle against human weakness would not have been complete without it. The Bible explains that he was made perfect by his sufferings (HEBREWS 2: 10). We are told that he 'was tempted *in every way that we are* but did not sin.' (HEBREWS 4: 15, TEV.) Torture, unhappily, is a not-uncommon feature of life. A complete man simply has to be acquainted with it.

Whenever followers of Jesus have been tortured, the temptation for them to escape by renouncing their faith has been enormous. But they have always been able to grit their teeth and say, 'He suffered torture willingly for my sake. Now I must try and stick it out for his sake. And since he has been through it himself and knows what it is like, he is sure to answer my prayers for help.'

As the apostle Peter wrote to the early Christians when they were being persecuted:

'If you endure suffering even when you have done right, God will bless you for it. It was to this that God called you; because *Christ himself suffered for you and left you an example*, so that you would follow in his steps.' (1 PETER 2: 20,21, TEV.)

Sin is Serious

The second reason for the crucifixion can only be explained by using an old-fashioned word: sin. There is a double wall around our prison. The inner wall is labelled 'sin', and the outer one, 'death'. The two are linked together with an unbreakable law, 'The wages of sin is death.' (ROMANS 6: 23.)

'Sin' is a word with several shades of meaning. Any single act of disobedience to God is a sin. But sin is also a Bible name for the weakness and perversity of human nature.

We are like drug addicts, completely hooked on sin. We can't stop sinning however hard we try. That is why the inner wall of our prison is called sin.

Since we can't conquer it ourselves we are utterly dependent upon God to cure us of our addiction to sin. If we co-operate with Him, God is willing to forgive us our sin as a first step towards freeing us from it. But the act of forgiveness carries with it a great danger, as the following story shows.

My friend Ralph owns a small business. A few years ago he was almost ruined by an unscrupulous employee. This man was in a position of trust, which he used to steal thousands of pounds from his employer.

When Ralph at last discovered what was happening the employee begged for mercy. He said he had yielded to temptation, but now he was terribly sorry and would make amends if only he could be given another chance.

With remarkable generosity Ralph forgave the man, and allowed him to keep his job. The result was disastrous. Within a year he was caught stealing from his employer again in a big way. And, sad to say, he blamed Ralph for this second lapse.

'He shouldn't have forgiven me so readily the first time,' he complained. 'Ralph made me feel that I hadn't really done him much harm, and so it didn't seem to matter very much if I twisted him again.'

The Bible reveals a wonderful understanding of human psychology. This is one of the many lines of evidence that the Bible is what it claims to be – a message from the all-wise Creator of man's body and mind.

There is no excuse for a Bible-reader making the same mistake as Ralph's dishonest employee. The Bible leaves us in no doubt whatever that sin is a very, very nasty business – even though God is willing to forgive it. The Bible tells us:

> 'By the death of Christ we are set free, and our sins are forgiven.' (EPHESIANS 1 : 7, TEV.)

So God is loving and merciful. He sets us free, and forgives us all our sins. Nevertheless, He has made it very plain that our sins are not just unimportant little slips. It was no light matter for God to free us and forgive us, since it cost Him the death of His only Son.

Clearly, this sinfulness of ours, from which God is willing to deliver us, must be a very terrible thing. If Christ died for this purpose, surely the least we can do is to fight tooth and nail against our own weaknesses in the future.

That is the second lesson of the cross. If we learn it, Christ will not have died in vain.

Freedom from Death

When Jesus smashed the inner wall of the prison, sin, then sooner or later the outer wall, death, was bound to go down also. As Peter said:

> 'God raised him up, having loosed the pangs of death, because it was not possible for him to be held by it.' (ACTS 2 : 24.)

That is the third great reason for the crucifixion. Jesus died so that death could be conquered.

To put it another way, his crucifixion tells the world that human nature deserves death; his resurrection from the dead is a proclamation that obedience to God leads to everlasting life.

Don't make the mistake of underrating the evidence for Christ's resurrection. One scholar has described it as the best attested fact in history. This may be a slight over-statement, but there really is a great deal of evidence that this miracle actually took place.

We now possess copies of the Gospels, or at least por-tions of them, written during the second century. Scholars agree that the originals of the Gospels must have been written during the first century, whilst eye-witnesses of the crucifixion were still alive.

If the resurrection stories had been false, those eye-witnesses would have refuted them. *But they didn't*. Why not? Surely because they knew them to be true.

The very existence of the Christian faith is difficult to account for, unless Christ rose from the dead. The first-century Christians who set the world ablaze with their message were highly unpopular. First the Jews tried to suppress them. Then, as the church began to grow, the Romans savagely opposed them.

But the early disciples sacrificed their lives to overcome this fierce opposition. Why? Their own explanation is this: they were eyewitnesses not only to a crucifixion, but to a miraculous resurrection, too.

These men were not fools. The circumstances they describe were such as to rule out all possibility of hallu-cination on their part. They were at first highly sceptical of the resurrection, until eventually they were convinced by 'many proofs' that the Lord really was alive again. (ACTS 1 : 3.)

Those early witnesses of Christ's resurrection knew what they were talking about. It makes sense to believe them.

Through the Broken Wall

This, then, is more Great News for the World. One human being has burst out of the prison. He conquered sin, and because of that he conquered death as well. Then he ascended to heaven, to wait until the time was ripe for his second coming.

Meanwhile there is hope for our imprisoned race. Where he led, we can follow if we wish. The path through the breach in the prison wall is not easy, but we do not have to tread it on our own. He assures us:

'Lo, I am with you always, to the close of the age.' (MATTHEW 28: 20.)

6

THE DOTTED LINE

A contract between two people is always treated as a very serious matter.

In some countries contracts are still made by the ancient method, in which the two parties make solemn declarations in the presence of witnesses: 'I promise to let Abdul graze his sheep on my land for the next 12 months.' 'And in return I promise to give Hassan the fruit of my three best palm trees at the next harvest.'

In the modern world contracts are usually made in writing, by signing on the dotted line. Yet almost everywhere the old method still lingers on, in connection with the most solemn contract that any two human beings can make together: 'I, John Doe, take thee, Rachel Roe, to be my lawful wedded wife.'

The importance of this decision to bind oneself for life to another human being cannot be overrated. But even so there is one decision that is more important still: the decision to follow Christ.

In the early days of Christianity this was not a decision to be rushed or made lightly. People knew then that becoming a Christian was the most vital and far-reaching decision that any person could possibly make.

It inevitably meant big changes in a person's life-style. It often meant unpopularity and financial loss, and could easily lead to suffering, imprisonment, or even death – just as it can today in some totalitarian countries. And it was not just a lifelong matter; it was concerned with eternity.

In those days a man first weighed up the consequences very carefully indeed, and then he made his solemn con-

tract with God. That is why the New Testament sometimes calls the Christian faith the 'covenant'[1] – an old
word for contract.

Making the Contract

The Bible shows us very clearly how those early converts
sealed their contract with God. For instance, the apostle
Peter spoke of:

> '... baptism, which now saves you, not by washing off
> bodily dirt, but by *the promise made to God* from a
> good conscience.' (1 PETER 3: 21, TEV.)

Thus it was in the act of Christian baptism that men and
women made their solemn promise to follow Christ. They
knew what this act meant; after baptism their whole lives
would be bound to change. As Paul put it:

> 'By our baptism, then, we were buried with him
> (Christ) and shared his death, in order that, just as
> Christ was raised from death by the glorious power of
> the Father, so also we might *live a new life*.' (ROMANS
> 6: 4, TEV.)

There is much to be learnt from that verse. To begin
with, note that baptism was described as a kind of 'burial'.
This, of course, stems from the fact that only one form of
baptism was known in those days. People being baptized
were placed for an instant beneath the surface of a body of
water. It was like being buried in water, just for a brief
moment.

There was a good reason for this. The form that baptism
took was full of meaning. Look back at the verse quoted
above. It shows that the person being baptized was expected to say to himself something like this:

'Christ willingly gave up his life. God then rewarded
him; He raised him up to a new kind of life, a far more

wonderful kind of life – everlasting life. In a smaller way, this applies to me, too. If I willingly surrender my life to God, He will give me a far better life, one day.

'So what I am going to do now is to demonstrate these facts, by acting out a sort of parable. As I go under the water the old *me* is going to die and be buried. But as I rise out of the water a new *ME* is going to be born. From now on the Lord Jesus Christ will help me to make my life more like his.'

Belief and Repentance

It stands to reason that you cannot make a contract with God unless you believe in Him. You also need to understand the terms of the contract, and to believe in them. So it is not surprising that the early Christians all had to reach a firm conviction before they could be baptized, as the following incidents show.

'When they (the Samaritan converts) believed Philip as he preached good news about the kingdom of God and the name of Jesus Christ, they were baptized, both men and women.' (ACTS 8: 12.)

'They (Paul and Silas) spoke the word of the Lord to him (the Philippian jailer) and to all that were in his house . . . he was baptized at once, with all his family . . . and he rejoiced with all his household that he had believed in God.' (ACTS 16: 32,34.)

But believing is not much use unless it leads to action. This is why belief has to be accompanied by what the Bible calls repentance, before a person can be baptized. Peter's words to the men and women of Jerusalem show this:

'When they heard this they were cut to the heart, and said to Peter and the rest of the apostles, "Brethren, what shall we do?" And Peter said to them, "*Repent, and be baptized every one of you for the forgiveness of your sins.*" ' (ACTS 2 : 37,38.)

These people obviously believed what Peter had been teaching, or they would not have been 'cut to the heart' by it. But that was not enough. Action was called for on their part. They were told first to repent and then to be baptized.

The word 'repent' means 'be sorry'. Not just *feel* sorry, but really *be* sorry. In other words, accept responsibility for the wrong that one has done in the past, and determine to do better in the future.

In the early church nobody was baptized until they showed clear signs of belief and repentance.

Forgiveness and Salvation

It takes two to make a contract. Each party to the contract makes a promise, or several promises, to the other party.

It is like this with baptism. We make our promises to turn away from the old self-centred way of life and start a new Christ-centred life. At the same time God makes two promises to us.

The first of these God fulfils immediately. He grants a blessing so wonderful that it brings an indescribable sense of relief. At the very moment of baptism He forgives all our past sins, so that we can start our new life in Christ with a clean sheet.

'Repent and be baptized every one of you *for the forgiveness of your sins.*' (ACTS 2 : 38.)

'Rise and be baptized and *wash away your sins.*' (ACTS 22 : 16.)

God's second promise starts to take effect at once, but it takes much longer to work out completely. He promises to watch over us night and day, to take charge of our lives, to help us grow more and more like His Son, and at last to give us everlasting life.

The Bible calls this continuing process 'salvation'. Because it begins at baptism Peter says 'baptism *now* saves you' (1 PETER 3: 21), while Jesus promises that 'he who believes and is baptized will be saved.' (MARK 16: 16.)

But the process of salvation cannot be completed until Christ comes again, when he will give everlasting life to those who have grown fit for it. Hence the New Testament also speaks of salvation as something we must wait for.

'Christ, having been offered once to bear the sins of many, will appear a second time . . . to save those who are eagerly waiting for him.' (HEBREWS 9: 28.)

Religious Inflation

We are all familiar with inflation. Governments keep printing more and more money. Workers receive more and more money in their pay packets. At the same time the real value of money keeps falling, and so nobody is any better off. Everyone agrees that inflation is a bad thing.

Something very much like that has happened in connection with Christianity. In New Testament times there was only a small number of Christians. But they all knew what Christianty really meant; they believed in it, they had shown repentance and been baptized. They were few in number, but their quality was high.

Today the reference books state that there are hundreds of millions of Christians in the world. This does not mean that all those people follow Christ. Far from it. All it means is that they were christened when they were babies.

In many Catholic countries, like Spain and Argentina, nearly all the babies born each year are christened. Even in Protestant countries such as Britain and America a great many babies are still christened, often when their parents are not even churchgoers.

This certainly keeps the numbers up, but at a frightful

price. It is like the action of governments that keep printing extra banknotes. The result is religious inflation. It
leads to a gain in quantity, but only at the expense of
quality.

The christening of babies is sometimes referred to as
baptism. In fact it is nothing of the kind. Infant christening has very little connection with the ceremony called
baptism in the New Testament, which was only for grown-
up, repentant believers.

I have found it painful to write these strongly critical
words about a widespread custom. But I have felt obliged
to do so because many of the people who read this book
will have been christened as babies. If you are one of them,
may I give you some friendly advice?

Look at the New Testament to see what it says about the
christening of babies. You will see that it says precisely
nothing. It treats infant christening as if it did not exist.

And that, if you are wise, is how you will regard your
own christening. Disregard it completely. It is not part of
God's religion, but just a man-made substitute.

You still need to make your own personal contract with
Jesus, to sign on the dotted line, so to speak, in the water
of baptism.

Faith

So far in this chapter the word faith has not appeared.
Instead you will find the word 'believe', which occurs in
several Bible verses telling us we must believe and be baptized.

In the English language we make a distinction between
'faith' and 'belief'. Sometimes you might even hear somebody say, 'I don't believe that such-and-such Christian *belief* is really true. I suppose I shall just have to accept it on
faith.'

If you were to translate that statement into Greek, the
language of the New Testament, it would read like a piece
of nonsense. This is because, in Greek, there is only one

word which means both 'belief' and 'faith'. To the early Christians, faith and belief were exactly the same thing.

So there can be no question of having faith in something you don't really believe. Faith *is* belief. Faith consists of believing that there is a God, that He has made some wonderful promises centred in His Son Jesus Christ, and that He will certainly keep them. As the Bible says:

> 'To have faith is to be *sure* of the things we hope for, to be *certain* of the things we cannot see.' (HEBREWS 11:1, TEV.)

One other thing. Faith involves hanging on to your convictions through thick and thin.

It may be easy to believe when the sun is shining and you have just had a pay rise. But God asks you to keep on believing when your husband has pneumonia and your child has just been run over. That's what faith means.

Here is an example of real faith. The apostle Paul wrote the following passage when he was a prisoner in chains:

> 'How great is the joy I have in my life in the Lord! . . . I have learned to be satisfied with what I have. I know what it is to be in need, and what it is to have more than enough. . . . I have the strength to face all conditions by the power that Christ gives me.'
> (PHILIPPIANS 4:10–13, TEV.)

How to Develop Faith

It is easy to admire Paul's wonderful faith. Trying to show the same kind of faith ourselves when the going is rough is a very different matter.

But don't be downhearted. Faith develops slowly, just like muscles and intelligence. Rome was not built in a day, and neither was Paul's attitude to his Roman prison. It was the outcome of a whole lifetime spent in faith-developing activities.

There are three of these: praying, reading and doing.

They are all very important. Do not settle for only one or two of them. If you want to grow strong in faith you should aim at practising all three, every day.

Prayer

The ability to pray is one of God's great gifts to man. It is one thing that distinguishes man from the animals. Never say, 'I can't pray.' You can. You were made in God's own image. Your prayer-power may have become rusty for want of use, but it is still there. With patience you will find you can get it going again.

People often say, 'But how can I pray if I have no faith?' But that is looking at the problem from the wrong end. It is better to ask, 'How can I expect to have faith if I do not pray?'

Perhaps you would like to pray but feel you can't, because you do not believe in God. Then take a good look into your own mind. Are you *absolutely certain* that there is no God? Because, if so, then you are a very unusual person!

Much more probably you would say, 'I really don't know if there is a God or not', or, 'No, I don't think there is a God – but, of course, you can't be sure.'

Either way, it means that your unbelief is not total. There is, so to speak, a mixture of unbelief and belief within you. At the very least there are a few shreds of belief – or faith – deep down in your unbelieving mind.

So it is clear what you need to do. Summon up whatever scraps of faith you may have, and just for a moment push the great waves of unbelief into the back of your mind. Then use your little bit of faith to utter a prayer. Be like the man who came to Jesus and said, 'I believe; help my unbelief!' (MARK 9: 24.)

That man realized that belief and unbelief were fighting for possession of his mind. He acted wisely. He used such belief as he possessed to ask the Lord Jesus for help.

If you have only a tiny crumb of faith as big as a grain

of seed, that's enough to start with, says Jesus. (LUKE 17 : 6.) God makes small seeds grow into great plants, and He will make your faith grow if you ask Him.

Bible Reading

No doubt you know at least one person who loves talking. He (or she) just goes on and on and on, always talking, never letting anyone else get a word in edgeways.

He doesn't care whether you have anything to say. He is interested only in himself. In short, he is a bore.

Very few people seem to realize that God probably dislikes bores as much as we do. Millions of people who never read the Bible pray to God every day. They expect God to listen to them, but they act as if they could not care less about the things God has to say to them.

This is not good enough. God has established two-way communication between heaven and earth, and He expects us to use it. He wants us to talk to Him and to listen, to pray and also to read His Word, the Bible.

Ignoring the Bible is so obviously a discourtesy to God. But that is less than half the trouble. By not reading the Bible we are depriving ourselves of a tremendous aid to faith. Consider these two sayings of Paul:

'Faith is awakened by the message, and the message that awakens it comes through the word of Christ.'
(ROMANS 10 : 17, NEB.)

'You have known the Holy Scriptures, which are able to give you the wisdom that leads to salvation through faith in Christ Jesus.' (2 TIMOTHY 3 : 15, TEV.)

'The message.' – The word of Christ. – 'The Holy Scriptures.' These – which today we should call, 'The Bible' – are what will give us faith, says Paul.

This is just plain commonsense. Faith is belief, and belief is based on knowledge, and the knowledge of God's ways comes from reading the Bible. *Of course* Bible read-ing will help us to develop faith.

Try it for yourself. To begin with, read just one chapter a' day – every day.² Read it carefully and thoughtfully, praying that God will help you to understand and to remember its message.

After a few months of this you will probably marvel at the difference it has made to you.

Doing God's Will

There is no substitute for practice. You will never be any good as a footballer, a musician, a swimmer, a dressmaker, an artist, or anything else you can think of, unless you are prepared to work at it.

This goes for developing faith, too. Jesus said:

'Whoever is willing to do what God wants will know whether what I teach comes from God or whether I speak on my own authority.' (JOHN 7: 17, TEV.)

Look closely at that promise. It applies to anyone who is 'willing to do what God wants'. How does a man show his willingness? Obviously by making an honest attempt at doing it.

The last part of the verse tells us what those willing doers can expect to receive. They will be given a clear answer to the question, 'Is Jesus the Son of God? Or is he an impostor?'

The advice of Jesus amounts to this. If you doubt whether Christianity is true, the best thing to do is to give it a trial. Try acting like one of Christ's disciples for a while – praying, reading, giving, helping, and being honest and upright in all your dealings.

Soon you will find what you are looking for: the con-viction that you ought to be a follower of Jesus Christ, the Son of God.

And by that time it will be a joy to you to become one.

7

INTO THE UNKNOWN

I grew up between the two world wars in the wheat-growing area of East Anglia. To us schoolboys one of the high-spots in the calendar was the day when Farmer Bennet threshed his corn.

It was before the days of combine harvesters, so the wheat was cut by a reaping machine and left lying in bundles about the field. When it was reasonably dry these were made into large stacks, to await the day when Farmer Bennet could hire a steam-driven threshing machine.

Then the fun began. As the farmer's men steadily dismantled the stack, a ring of boys and dogs waited expectantly. Every so often a rat would break out of the stack and dash for cover, with wildly excited boys and yelping dogs in hot pursuit.

Meanwhile the threshing machine banged away at the sheaves of corn. A steady stream of grain poured into the waiting sacks, whilst another part of the machine disgorged a second stream. This was the useless part of the ears of the corn, called chaff. A bonfire was kept burning all day long to get rid of it.

Scenes something like this, but with an ox's hooves and a winnowing tool doing the work instead of a machine, were common in the days of Jesus Christ. Some of his parables were based upon such events. So were the words of John the Baptist, who said about Jesus:

'He has his winnowing-shovel with him, to thresh out all the grain; he will gather his wheat into his barn, but burn the chaff in a fire that never goes out!'

(MATTHEW 3: 12, TEV.)

A Leap into the Darkness

For many people death is a terrifying leap into the unknown. Even in this unbelieving age a great many people believe there must be some sort of conscious existence after death, but few of them have any clear idea of what to expect.

This uncertainty is quite unnecessary, since the Bible tells us all the essential facts about life and death. Unfortunately many people refuse to face the most basic fact of all, because the Bible's teaching on this point is highly unpalatable. It tells us that life after death is *only* for those who earnestly follow Christ. Everybody else will be wiped out of existence. They are like the chaff in the passage quoted above; the chaff is useless and the farmer does not want it cluttering up his farmyard, so he burns it to get it out of the way.

People who have not learned to enjoy walking in God's ways are misfits in God's world. They are physically incapable of finding everlasting happiness in God's presence. The kindest thing God can do to them is to let them cease to exist, just as men destroy chaff, and weeds, and wrecked cars.

So the Bible warns us again and again that, unless we allow God to make us fit for everlasting happiness, He will have to destroy us.

'The Lord preserves all who love Him, but all the wicked will He *destroy*.' (PSALM 145: 20.)

'He who despises the word brings *destruction* upon himself, but he who respects the commandment will be rewarded.' (PROVERBS 13: 13.)

'Enter by the narrow gate; for the gate is wide and the way is easy, that leads to *destruction*, and those who enter by it are many. For the gate is narrow and the way is hard, that leads to life, and those who find it are few.' (MATTHEW 7: 13,14.)

'Those who do not obey the gospel of our Lord Jesus
... shall suffer the punishment of eternal *destruction*
and exclusion from the presence of the Lord and from
the glory of his might, when he comes on that day to be
glorified in his saints.' (2 THESSALONIANS 1:9,10.)

In each of those four quotations there is a picture of
mankind sorting itself into two classes. There are those
who learn to co-operate with God; they will ultimately
find everlasting life in his presence. The rest of mankind –
the great majority – are unsuitable for God's eternal pur-
poses; the only appropriate fate for them is destruction.

The Real Hell Fire

Jesus loved to speak in parables, using familiar scenes as
vivid illustrations of the things he taught.

One of those he used was a gruesome scene. Just outside
the old city of Jerusalem was the municipal rubbish
dump, in the bottom of a valley called Gehenna. It was
a most revolting place. Not only was the city's rubbish
and sewage tipped there, but the bodies of executed criminals were denied a decent burial; they were flung into
Gehenna like so much human rubbish, to rot and breed
maggots, or perhaps to be burnt along with the other
rubbish.

Jesus spoke of Gehenna several times. Unfortunately his
meaning is distorted in most English Bibles, since translators usually put the English word 'hell' instead of the
Greek place-name 'Gehenna'.[1] Some translations, such as
the Revised Standard Version, supply a footnote explaining that Jesus actually said 'Gehenna', not 'hell'. Here is
one such passage.

'If your foot causes you to sin, cut it off; it is better for
you to enter life lame than with two feet to be thrown
into Gehenna. And if your eye causes you to sin, pluck
it out; it is better for you to enter the kingdom of God
with one eye than with two eyes to be thrown into

Gehenna, where their worm does not die and the fire is not quenched.' (MARK 9: 45–48.)

Here we have undoubtedly the language of parable. Those who sacrifice a foot or an eye for Jesus will not *literally* enter everlasting life with only one foot or one eye, as this passage suggests! Nor will all those who disobey Jesus have their bodies literally thrown into Gehenna, to be eaten by worms (maggots) or destroyed by fire. What Jesus is really saying, in effect, is something like this:

'You know what men do with criminals that are not fit to live: they put them to death and then throw their bodies into Gehenna to be destroyed by worms or by fire. Well, that is an illustration of what God will do to all the people who are not fit to live for ever in His kingdom. He will destroy them as completely as we destroy the bodies of criminals. To avoid such a fate it is worth making great sacrifices.'

The Meaning of the Soul

There are two opposite ways of reacting to this teaching of Jesus. One – the right way – is to say, 'The situation is very serious. It looks as if I am on the easy road leading to destruction, to the total extinction of my life. I must do something about it, so as to cross over to the narrow road that leads to everlasting happiness.'

Unhappily, that healthy reaction is decidedly uncommon. There is a deep-rooted human instinct to defend one's present position, and a reluctance to admit that a change is necessary. People will go to almost any length to convince themselves that they are really all right: that death is not going to mean an abrupt end for themselves.

The favourite escape route is by juggling with the word 'soul'. There is a very common belief that we have inside us something called a soul, which goes on living when the body dies. This belief is popular because it is comforting. But it is the very opposite of what the Bible teaches.

In the Bible the word 'soul' is never used in that way.[2] Instead, it is used to mean 'person', or 'self', or 'life'. We still find it used in this way in everyday English, in expressions such as, 'Poor old soul (person)', 'Put your heart and soul (self) into the game', and 'SOS – save our souls [3] (lives)'.

The word 'soul' is used in many places in the King James Version of the Bible (published 1611) where more modern translations give us the real meaning. Here are three examples from the King James Version, with the words used in the Revised Standard Version (published 1952) in brackets.

'And the Lord God formed man of the dust of the ground, and breathed into his nostrils the breath of life; and man became a living soul (being).' (GENESIS 2: 7.)

'The Lord delivered Lachish into the hand of Israel, which . . . smote it with the edge of the sword, and all the souls (persons) that were therein.' (JOSHUA 10: 32.)

'The writing of Hezekiah king of Judah, when he had been sick, and was recovered of his sickness . . . "Thou hast in love to my soul (life) delivered it from the pit of corruption." ' (ISAIAH 38: 9,17.)

'Being', 'person', 'life'. This is how modern versions of the Bible often translate the Hebrew and Greek words for 'soul'. Here is one passage where modern translations usually stick to the old word, soul.

'The soul that sins *shall die*.' (EZEKIEL 18: 20.)

The meaning of all this is unmistakable. In the Bible, 'soul' does not refer to some sort of immortal spirit inside a person. *The soul is the person himself.*

And because the person – the soul – is sinful, the person dies. There is no 'inner man' left to live on when the body dies. Death really is the end of life, as the Bible clearly states in the following words:

'The dead know nothing . . . Their love and their hate
and their envy have already perished.'

(ECCLESIASTES 9 : 5,6.)

Sleeping and Waking Up

To make quite sure that we have got the message, the
Bible frequently refers to death as a 'sleep'. People who
are too busy to find time for God will die without any hope
of everlasting life; sooner or later they will fall into an
endless sleep. As the prophet says, 'They shall sleep a per-
petual sleep and not wake.' (JEREMIAH 51 : 57.)

But those who decide to centre their lives on the Lord
Jesus Christ are in a very different position. Death is still
a sleep, even to them, but a sleep with a difference. Their
death is a sleep which will be broken when Jesus comes to
wake them up, just as his own sleep in the tomb was ended
when God raised Jesus from the dead.

To demonstrate this wonderful fact the Lord Jesus
Christ raised a few disciples from the dead, when he was
on earth the first time. One of these was his friend Lazarus,
who fell ill and died. When Jesus heard the bad news he
said :

'Our friend Lazarus has fallen asleep, but I go to
awake him out of sleep.' (JOHN 11 : 11.)

John goes on to describe how the grave of Lazarus was
opened up. Jesus then called to the dead body in the tomb,
'Lazarus, come out' – and Lazarus walked out of his grave,
a living man once more.

What happened to Lazarus is only a foretaste of what
will happen to all Jesus's friends when he comes back to
the earth. Scripture is clear and emphatic about this :

'Since we believe that Jesus died and rose again, even
so, through Jesus, God will bring with him those who
have fallen asleep . . . the Lord himself will descend
from heaven . . . and *the dead in Christ will rise.*'

(1 THESSALONIANS 4 : 14–16.)

> 'Christ has been raised from the dead, the first fruits of those who have fallen asleep. For as by a man (Adam) came death, by a man (Christ) has come also the *resurrection of the dead*. . . . But each in his own order: Christ the first fruits, then at his coming those who belong to Christ.' (1 CORINTHIANS 15 : 20–23.)

All through the New Testament we find the same teaching. When the Lord Jesus Christ comes back to the earth he will raise his faithful followers from the dead, and give them everlasting life. This is the only way that anybody will ever find life beyond the grave. There is no other hope.

The Day of Judgment

It is not only the real friends of Jesus who will be raised from the dead. His false friends, as well as his outright enemies, will also be roused from the sleep of death to stand trial before the Son of God. Here are three of the many Bible verses that solemnly warn us about this.

> 'Many of those who sleep in the dust of the earth shall awake, some to everlasting life, and some to shame and everlasting contempt.' (DANIEL 12 : 2.)

> 'Christ Jesus who is to judge the living and the dead . . .' (2 TIMOTHY 4 : 1.)

> 'We must all appear before the judgment seat of Christ, so that each one may receive good or evil, according to what he has done in the body.'
>
> (2 CORINTHIANS 5 : 10.)

Thus all of us who have heard the call of Jesus will have to stand before him at that day. He will sort us into two groups, and his decisions will all be final; there will be no court of appeal.

Those who are no use to him will be destroyed as completely as the rubbish of Jerusalem that used to be thrown into Gehenna. As David said:

'Yet a little while, and the wicked will be no more;
Though you look well at his place, he will not be there.'
(PSALM 37 : 10.)

But the other group will be miraculously transformed
so that their bodies become the image of their Master's,
and fit to enter eternity. In the words of Paul:

'We eagerly wait for our Saviour to come from heaven,
the Lord Jesus Christ. He will change our weak mortal
bodies and make them like his own glorious body.'
(PHILIPPIANS 3 : 20,21, TEV.)

Inheriting the Earth

When the Lord Jesus Christ has made his faithful servants
immortal they will enter into everlasting life. It may come
as a surprise to learn that this is something they will enjoy
on earth.
On earth?
Yes, on earth. That is precisely what the Bible says.

'The righteous shall possess *the land* and shall live
there at peace *for ever*.' (PSALM 37 : 29, NEB.)

'Blessed are the meek, for they shall inherit *the earth*.'
(MATTHEW 5 : 5.)

'You (Jesus) bought men for God
From every tribe, and language, and people, and nation.
You have made them a kingdom of priests to serve our
God;
And they shall rule *on earth*.'
(REVELATION 5 : 9,10,TEV.)

There is a wonderful future in store for those who truly
give their lives to the Lord Jesus. There is a marvellous
future in store for this planet of ours, too, and the two are
intertwined.
In the next chapter we shall see how this is.

8

PLAN FOR A PLANET

Raymond's bewilderment is typical of many of my friends.

'Honestly, I don't know what to believe. When I look up at the trees and the birds and the mountains, or at the night sky, I feel as if there simply must be a God. How else could this marvellous universe have come about?

'Then, when I look down at this wretched world of ours, I can't help doubting. Just look at it: floods and famines and earthquakes and epidemics, thousands of little children starving to death every year, people being killed and maimed and blinded every day in wars or terrorist attacks or riots or bank raids, greed and cruelty everywhere.

'Does the world really have to be like this? Why is life so unfair? Surely, if there is a God in control of the world, He ought to be able to make a better job of it than this. Why doesn't He do something about it? Isn't He able to, or doesn't He care?'

World in a Mess

In a sense, the whole Bible is the only complete answer to these questions.[1] Very briefly, there are three main points to take into account.

First of all, the world is in a wretched condition only because man is sinful. It is no use blaming God for our own wickedness, even though He did give us the freedom to sin if we so choose. After all, nobody would want to surrender his free will, even if lots of men do abuse their freedom by making others suffer; none of us would wish to become a puppet or a robot!

The second point is that God has allowed the world to remain like this because He is doing a wonderful work in it. As we have seen in Chapters 4 to 7, He is busy fashioning characters that will be fit to live for ever and ever in perfect happiness. And a world filled with a mixture of joy and sorrow is the best possible place for developing such characters.

Finally, the present tragic state of the world is only temporary. It is rather like the pickle that your house is in when its interior is being repainted; you can put up with paintpots and ladders and dustsheets in your living room when you know that in a little while everything is going to be clean and tidy, and nicer than it has ever been before.

That is why the full Christian message is such Great News for the World. Raymond (like millions of other people) wanted to know why God doesn't do something about the state the world is in.

The answer comes shining out of the Bible as clear as a searchlight beam. There is no need to wonder or to worry, because God is going to do something about it – and very soon, too. That is precisely why Jesus Christ is coming back to the earth.

Clearing Up the Mess

About a quarter of a century ago the British people were called upon to elect a new parliament, at a time when Britain was facing grave difficulties.

It was widely believed that the politicians who had been ruling Britain for several years – let's call them the X Party – were responsible for the nation's troubles. So their principal opponents flooded the country with election posters promising, 'The Y Party will clear up the mess'.

The public believed this and voted them into office. But the Y Party failed to 'clear up the mess'. They had nothing like enough ability or power to do so.

Several British governments have come and gone since then, and things have gone from bad to worse. Although Britain and the other advanced nations are still enjoying

peace and prosperity they are like men living on the slopes
of a volcano, with the threat of disaster constantly over-
shadowing them. Meanwhile, the British public has grown
more cynical: it knows now that no politicians are able to
solve the appalling problems facing mankind.

It is not only Britain that is facing a crisis. Every country on earth is in trouble of some sort. The world as a
whole is in a ghastly mess, and its leaders have no real idea
how to clear it up.

For one thing, this is a job that cannot be tackled piece-
meal, each country acting on its own. The world today is
too small, too inter-related, for global problems to be
solved like that. What we obviously need is a worldwide
government, a good one, with both the ability and the
power to put things right. It would have to be headed by
some strong-minded, gifted individual capable of ruling
the entire planet, and ruling it well.

A pipe dream? On the face of it, so it would seem. There
is not a single man on earth who could measure up to such
a superhuman task. The only man who is qualified for the
job is in heaven – but he would certainly be the ideal man
for it if he were here.

*That is why the second coming of Christ is such Great
News for the World.*

King Jesus

Try to forget that you have ever seen any pictures of
Jesus. Nearly all of them are misleading. He was nothing
like the pale, insipid character with the butter-wouldn't-
melt-in-my-mouth expression that artists love to portray.

In actual fact he was a tremendously forceful personality. Though he was only a mortal man in those days, he
still had the strength of character to right some of the most
appalling wrongs of his time.

On one occasion he went into the temple of God in
Jerusalem, and found its great courtyard filled with shady
business men feathering their nests. Singlehanded, he de-

nounced their wickedness so effectively that not one of them could stand against him. They fled from the temple in confusion, knowing in their hearts that they were in the wrong and that here was a man with the personality and the power to put things right.

The way he cleaned up the temple then is a foretaste of the way he will clean up the worldwide mess when he comes again. God has already given him all the extra power he will need for such a gigantic task: 'All authority in heaven and on earth has been given unto me,' he announced after he rose from the dead. (MATTHEW 28: 18.)

A thousand years before he was born, the Old Testament foretold that a Son of God would become king of the world:

'You are my son (says God), today I have begotten you.
Ask of me, and I will make the nations your heritage,
   and the ends of the earth your possession.
You shall break them with a rod of iron,
   and dash them in pieces like a potter's vessel.'

                         (PSALM 2: 7–9.)

After he ascended to heaven the New Testament explained, in vivid picture-language, that he will come back to fulfil that prophecy:

'The kingdom of the world has become the kingdom of our Lord and of his Christ, and he shall reign for ever and ever . . .

'From his mouth there went a sharp sword with which to smite the nations; for it is he who shall rule them with an iron rod . . . And on his robe and on his thigh there was written the name: "King of kings and Lord of lords." ' (REVELATION 11: 15, RSV; 19: 15,16, NEB.)

The King and His Kingdom

The Bible has a name for the world as it will be when the Lord Jesus Christ has come back and is ruling over it: the

Kingdom of God. Jesus taught his disciples to pray for that kingdom:

> 'Pray then like this:
> "Our Father who art in heaven,
> Hallowed be thy name.
> *Thy kingdom come*,
> Thy will be done,
> On earth as it is in heaven..."'
>
> (MATTHEW 6: 9,10.)

He also told them exactly how, and when, that prayer would be answered: at his second coming.

> 'There will be signs in sun and moon and stars, and upon the earth distress of nations... And then they will see *the Son of man coming* in a cloud with power and great glory... when you see these things taking place, you know that *the kingdom of God is near.*'
>
> (LUKE 21: 25–31.)

Thus, when Christ rules over it the whole world will be God's kingdom. Christ will rule on behalf of his Father, so that there will be heavenly splendour right here. Already God's will is done in heaven; soon it will be done on earth, too.

The Bible gives many a glimpse of this coming kingdom. The rest of this chapter will reveal a few of them. As you read on, keep reminding yourself: 'This is our world as it will soon become – probably in our time!'

It *will* come about; that much is certain. Three thousand years of fulfilled prophecy is ample proof that God always keeps His promises.

A Ruler who Loves his people

The trouble with all ordinary rulers is that they love ruling more than they love their people. The British statesman, Lord Acton, had a lifetime's experience of politicians. He summed it up like this:

'Power tends to corrupt, and absolute power corrupts absolutely. Great men are almost always bad men.' [2]

If absolute power corrupts absolutely, the mere thought of one man ruling the whole world is enough to send icy shivers running up your spine. Happily, the Lord Jesus Christ is the one exception to the general pattern of human nature.

Read the four Gospels, and see how Jesus always put other people first and himself last. And he really was morally incorruptible. No other man has ever dared to ask a crowd, 'Which one of you can prove that I am guilty of sin?' or to declare, 'I always do what pleases him (God).' (JOHN 8: 46,29, TEV.)

So when Christ governs the world he will not just be a good ruler – he will be a *perfect* ruler. One prophet describes his reign like this:

'The Spirit of the Lord shall rest upon him,
    the spirit of wisdom and understanding,
    the spirit of counsel and might,
    the spirit of knowledge and the fear of the Lord,
And his delight shall be in the fear of the Lord.

'He shall not judge by what his eyes see,
    or decide by what his ears hear;
But with righteousness he shall judge the poor,
    and decide with equity for the meek of the earth.'
                                    (ISAIAH 11: 2–4.)

King David of Israel – a brilliant ruler himself – was full of admiration for this great future king.

'May all kings fall down before him, all nations serve
   him!
For he delivers the needy when he calls,
   the poor and him who has no helper.
He has pity on the weak and the needy,
   and saves the lives of the needy.
From oppression and violence he redeems their life;
   and precious is their blood in his sight.'

(PSALM 72: 11–14.)

Hundreds of millions today live bedraggled lives,
crushed by hopeless poverty, or oppressed by power-drunk
tyrants. Their misery will not last much longer. When
Christ rules the earth the welfare of the common people
will be his first concern.

Kind, but Firm

Does this mean that people will be able to do as they like
in the Kingdom of God? Far from it! Those who are prepared to serve God and love their neighbours will find the
Kingdom a delightful place, but those who want to live
selfishly or cruelly will be made to think again.

Yet this ruler's power will not grow out of the barrel of
a gun. With God Almighty behind him the Lord Jesus will
have better methods of keeping rebels under control, as
these two quotations show:

'The Lord will become king over all the earth ... And
if any of the families of the earth do not go up to Jerusalem to worship the King, the Lord of hosts, there will be
no rain upon them.'

(ZECHARIAH 14: 9,17.)

'He (Christ) shall judge the poor with justice
   and defend the humble in the land with equity;
His mouth shall be a rod to strike down the ruthless,
   and with a sword he shall slay the wicked ...

'They (his subjects) shall not hurt or destroy in all my
    holy mountain;
For as the waters fill the sea,
    so shall the land be filled with the knowledge of the
    Lord.'

(ISAIAH 11: 4,9, NEB.)

There are not likely to be many complaints about these
very effective methods of policing the world. Most people
will be only too glad to see the end of vandalism, hooli-
ganism and crime. There will be widespread approval for
a world-state where Article No. 1 in the Constitution is,
'Thou shalt love the Lord thy God, and thy neighbour as
thyself.' As the prophet says:

'In his days shall the righteous flourish;
And abundance of peace, till the moon be no more ...
And men shall be blessed in him;
All nations shall call him happy.'

(PSALM 72: 7,17, RV.)

Peace and Plenty

To see what a crazy society modern man has built up, look
at the way the world's great army of research scientists is
employed. Only a small minority of them are busy trying
to improve the quality of human life.

Many more are beavering away at projects of doubtful
value to mankind, ranging all the way from inventing
striped toothpaste to landing men on the moon. But the
crowning obscenity is this: no less than half the research
scientists in the world are concerned with what is politely
termed 'defence' – in other words, with wholesale death
and destruction.

This incredible folly will soon come to an end. Jesus
Christ was not named 'Prince of Peace' for nothing; nor
were the angels mistaken when they sang, 'On earth peace
among men', the day he was born. (ISAIAH 9: 6; LUKE

2 : 14.) In his kingdom this bloodstained planet of ours will at last be freed from the curse of war.

'The battle bow shall be cut off,
    and *he shall command peace to the nations.*
His dominion shall be from sea to sea,
    and from the River to the ends of the earth.'

                          (ZECHARIAH 9 : 10.)

'Out of Zion shall go forth the law,
    and the word of the Lord from Jerusalem.
He shall judge between many peoples,
    and shall decide for strong nations afar off;
And they shall beat their swords into ploughshares,
    and their spears into pruning hooks;
Nation shall not lift up sword against nation,
    neither shall they learn war any more;
But they shall sit every man under his vine and under
      his fig tree,
    and none shall make them afraid.'

                          (MICAH 4 : 2–4.)

When the world's resources are no longer squandered on weapons of war, poverty will be a thing of the past. With the Son of God controlling the world's agriculture there will be no world shortage of food.

Above all, he will ensure that supplies are fairly distributed. To the everlasting shame of our so-called 'Western Christian Civilisation', there are millions of overfed white men and women today spending more on slimming aids than many black or brown people are able to spend on food. It won't be like that in the Kingdom of God:

'Behold, the days are coming, says the Lord,
    when the ploughman shall overtake the reaper,
    and the treader of grapes him who sows the seed;
The mountains shall drip sweet wine,
    and all the hills shall flow with it.'

                          (AMOS 9 : 13.)

'There shall be abundance of corn in the earth upon
    the top of the mountains;
The fruit thereof shall shake like Lebanon:
And they of the city shall flourish like grass of the
    earth.'

(PSALM 72: 16, RV.)

Health and Happiness

When the Son of God was on the earth before, he gave
mankind a preview of what is coming. By the power of his
Father he healed the sick, the lame, the blind and the deaf.
So did his immediate associates.

When he reigns as King of the World, all this will be
repeated on a global scale. The result will be worldwide
happiness, such as men could not begin to hope for apart
from him:

'The wilderness and the dry land shall be glad,
    the desert shall rejoice and blossom;
Like the crocus it shall blossom abundantly,
    and rejoice with joy and singing ...

'Then the eyes of the blind shall be opened,
    and the ears of the deaf unstopped;
Then shall the lame man leap like a hart,
    and the tongue of the dumb sing for joy ...

'And the ransomed of the Lord shall return,
    and come to Zion with singing;
Everlasting joy shall be upon their heads;
    they shall obtain joy and gladness,
    and sorrow and sighing shall flee away.'

(ISAIAH 35: 1,2,5,6,10.)

Even the power of death will be weakened, since the
span of mortal life will be greatly prolonged:

'No more shall be heard in it the sound of weeping
    and the cry of distress.

No more shall there be in it
    an infant that lives but a few days,
    or an old man who does not fill out his days,
For the child shall die an hundred years old,
    and the sinner a hundred years old shall be accursed.
They shall build houses and inhabit them;
    they shall plant vineyards and eat their fruit.
They shall not build and another inhabit;
    they shall not plant and another eat;
For like the days of a tree shall the days of my people
    be,
    and my chosen shall long enjoy the work of their
    hands.'

(ISAIAH 65 : 19–22.)

Mortals and Immortals

One very important point must now be emphasised. *There will be two sorts of people in the Kingdom of God, mortals and immortals.*

There will, in fact, be a three-tier structure in the Kingdom, like this:

JESUS CHRIST,
THE IMMORTAL KING

HIS IMMORTAL HELPERS

MULTITUDES OF ORDINARY, FLESH-AND-BLOOD,
MORTAL MEN AND WOMEN — THE CITIZENS OF THE KINGDOM

There is no doubt that the Kingdom will be inhabited by ordinary flesh-and-blood people. Nearly all the Scriptures quoted in this chapter speak of such folk enjoying

life under Christ's worldwide rule. Look back at them and
see.

They tell of people who beat swords into ploughshares,
who bring up children, who plant vines and fig trees, sow
seeds and make wine, suffer illness and rejoice in being
cured. These people live to a great old age (as long as
trees), but not for ever. They are greatly blessed and very
happy – but they are still mortal men and women.

It is not difficult to see where these mortal people come
from. When Christ returns there will be vast numbers of
people living who have never had the opportunity to follow him. For example, there are hundreds of millions in
China and Moslem countries today who might never even
see a Bible before Christ comes back.

If they survive until Christ is on the earth again, their
turn will come then. They and their descendants will be
the happiest mortal men and women to walk this earth
since Adam and Eve were expelled from Eden.

As the flesh-and-blood inhabitants of God's Kingdom
they will enjoy many blessings. Above all, they will have
a great opportunity to serve God faithfully, and eventually
to find everlasting life. To help them, God will provide
expert teachers – immortal teachers, in fact.

Those immortal teachers will be what you might call the
'ruling class' in the Kingdom of God. *And you can become
one of them, if you wish,* because this is the Christian
hope of everlasting life as the Bible portrays it.

There is something very fitting about this. True Christianity involves (among other things) loving and helping
one's fellow men. It is only reasonable that those who do
this faithfully in this life should be allowed the joy of
doing it on a higher level in the age to come. As the Bible
says:

'If we have died with him (Christ) we shall also live
with him; if we endure, *we shall also reign with him.*'
(2 TIMOTHY 2: 12.)

'As my Father appointed a kingdom for me, so do I appoint for you that you may eat and drink at my table in my kingdom, and *sit on thrones judging the twelve tribes of Israel.*' (LUKE 22 : 29,30.)

'Don't you know that God's people will *judge the world*?' (1 CORINTHIANS 6: 2, TEV.)

'Blessed and holy is he who shares in the first resurrection! Over such the second death has no power, but they shall be priests of God and of Christ, and *they shall reign with him* a thousand years.' (REVELATION 20: 6.)

Everlasting Joy

Don't underestimate the joy involved in helping Christ to rule the world. After all, what are the main ingredients of human happiness?

Security; peace of mind; freedom from fear and from suffering; and, above all, worthwhile work to do.

The men and women who are given everlasting life in God's Kingdom will find all those things in abundance. Their immortal bodies will be incapable of sinning, or of feeling pain. They will no longer make foolish mistakes and regret them bitterly, but everything they do will be in harmony with the all-wise will of their God.

And their work will be of the most rewarding kind imaginable. The mortal inhabitants of the Kingdom will be in constant need of help and guidance, and their immortal rulers will find immense satisfaction in leading them along the uphill road to immortality.

Eventually the immortals will see the fruit of their labours. After a long period God will make another great change in the state of the world. Those mortals that are worthy will themselves be made immortal, and the rest will be destroyed.

Then there will be no more fallen human nature upon the earth, no more sin, no more death. God's plan will have reached its climax; Jesus will hand over his kingdom to his Father, and God Himself will dwell in every immortal being.[3]

But that is all a long way off – more than a thousand years in the future, in fact. It is enough to keep that picture in the back of our minds as the ultimate destiny of our planet.

The prayer, 'Thy kingdom come', tells us where to concentrate our thoughts at present. The world desperately needs the Lord's return, and that should be our hearts' desire today. As Peter says:

'What kind of people should you be? Your lives should be holy and dedicated to God, as you wait for the Day of God, and do your best to make it come soon.' (2 Peter 3: 11,12, TEV.)

9

AN ANCIENT FAITH IN MODERN DRESS

When I was a young man I used to spend many a Saturday afternoon at Speakers' Corner in London's Hyde Park. One day I met there a man who had lost all faith in God.

'You'll never make a Christian of me,' he said, emphatically. 'Never!'

'Why not? What have you got against Christianity?' I asked.

'I was put off it for life during World War I, when my Indian batman opened my eyes to the absurdity of it all. "What funny people you Europeans are," he said. "You send missionaries to India to tell us ignorant people to follow Christ and to love one another. Then when a war breaks out you pay us to come to France and help the English Christians to kill the German Christians."

'I never went to church again after Mohammed Khan said that. How could I? Every church in Europe supported its own side during the war. You would hear men praying for strength before they went over the top. Then they would charge and say, "God help me," to themselves as they stuck a bayonet into the other fellow, who, as likely as not, was praying to the same God at the same time.'

I had to agree with him that this was indeed a terrible state of affairs. Nevertheless, he was making a slight overstatement. It was not true that 'every church in Europe' supported its own side during the war.

Several churches, I told him, made a firm stand during both world wars for what is loosely termed 'Christian pacifism'. (So also did many individuals in other communities.) Most of these base their convictions on the simple belief that their Master meant what he said, in New Testament passages like this:

> 'I say to you (said Jesus), Do not resist one who is evil. But if any one strikes you on the right cheek, turn to him the other also . . . if any one forces you to go one mile, go with him two miles . . . Love your enemies and pray for those who persecute you.' (MATTHEW 5 : 39–44.)

Prominent among the churches that have always tried to follow this difficult teaching is the body I belong to, the Christadelphians. I shall spend the rest of this chapter explaining why we do this, and what we think practical Christianity is meant to be like.

The Verdict of Historians

Bertrand Russell, the philosopher and historian, was an unbeliever. From this neutral point of view he studied both the Christians of the first century and the Christian sects of the twentieth century, and came up with the following conclusion:

> 'Christianity was, in its earliest days, entirely unpolitical. The best representatives of the primitive tradition in our time are the Christadelphians, who believe the end of the world to be imminent, and refuse to have any part or lot in secular affairs.' [1]

In other words, Christianity in its earliest form was very different from what is generally regarded as Christianity today. And the Christadelphians (despite our many failings, which we would be the first to admit) have come closer to the first-century idea of a Christian church than any other community, says Russell.

His conclusion was shared by another independent scholar, Prof. G. C. Field. He was appointed by the British Government during World War II to sit on what was known as a conscientious objectors tribunal. This was a legal body whose job was to sit in judgment on men who refused to bear arms because of their beliefs.

After the war he published a book describing his experiences on this legal tribunal. In it he wrote:

> 'If we are to obey in detail the injunctions that were given to the first Christians, we must put ourselves in the same position as the first Christians, and regard ourselves as a small band of believers, living in a world that as a whole has not accepted Christ, following the path of separation and taking no responsibility for the affairs of this world . . . This is the line actually followed by some of the smaller Christian sects, such as the Christadelphians and the Plymouth Brethren . . . I feel little doubt that *their attitude is much closer to the attitude of the earliest Christians than that of the larger religious bodies.*' [2] (My italics.)

Bible-Based Christianity

Russell and Field were both very perceptive men. They appear to have realised that the whole aim of the Christadelphians is to recapture, as closely as is humanly possible, the beliefs and the practices of the early church. We may not have succeeded in this as well as we should have liked, but at least there are some independent observers who think we are heading in the right direction.

Unlike this chapter, which is concerned with Christian living, the previous chapters of this book have set out to show what the first-century Christians really believed – and consequently what we ought to believe today.

One thing about these earlier chapters is almost sure to have struck you: the Bible has been quoted a great deal. This is typical of the Christadelphian approach to religion. First-century Christianity was thoroughly Bible-based, and so we try to make our faith like that, too.

For this reason every earnest Christadelphian reckons to

read a portion of the Bible every day. This is no empty ritual; we think deeply about what we read, and find lessons in it. The Bible to us is a powerhouse, the Spirit of God in written form, on tap for our daily use.

Following Christ is often a hard struggle. The would-be disciple soon finds that his own strength is not enough. We read the Bible for the same reason that we pray: we need heavenly strength to help us on the way, and the Bible and prayer are the twin sources of that strength.

Some Fallacies Exploded

It might be useful at this point to say what we are not.

To begin with we are not, as one enquirer put it, 'One of them new-fangled American sects.' Only a small minority of the world's Christadelphians are Americans. Although the actual name Christadelphian was coined in America in 1864 there are records of churches holding Christadelphian beliefs in various European countries long before that.

For as long as anyone can remember there have been more Christadelphians in England than anywhere else in the world. Today there are some three hundred Christadelphian meetings in Britain, and smaller numbers in about two dozen other countries scattered across the five continents.

Neither are we one of those sects that claim a monopoly of religious wisdom. No Christadelphian teacher has ever claimed to be inspired. All we would ever dare to say is something like this:

'Look, this is what I have learnt from reading my Bible carefully. Perhaps if you read your Bible with an open mind you might come to much the same conclusions. Let's have a chat about it and see if we can't reach agreement.'

Finally, we don't pretend to know all the answers. We are painfully aware that all human beings make mistakes, ourselves included. There are a number of difficult passages in the Bible that, try as we will, we have never been able to understand completely. When the Lord returns we shall ask him to explain them. Until then, we are glad to recognise our own limitations.

Christian Fellowship

The night before he was crucified Jesus had a meal with his disciples. As the apostle Paul explained in the words quoted below, Jesus used that meal to institute a simple ceremony, by which his followers were ever after to remember him.

> 'The Lord Jesus on the night when he was betrayed took bread, and when he had given thanks, he broke it, and said, "This is my body which is for you. *Do this in remembrance of me.*" In the same way also the cup, after supper, saying, "This cup is the new covenant in my blood. *Do this, as often as you drink it, in remembrance of me.*" ' (1 CORINTHIANS 11 : 23–25.)

This little ceremony in memory of their Lord's death was held by the early disciples on the first day of each week.[3] Consequently, the heart of the regular Christadelphian meeting for worship on Sunday is always this same act of communion, or fellowship, as the New Testament calls it.

It is in fact a double act of fellowship. It signifies our union with God, and our union with our fellow believers, too. For the Christadelphian it is a reminder that all true believers are really one big family.

The very name Christadelphian also reminds him of this. It is derived from a phrase in the Greek New Testament which is translated 'Brethren in Christ'. (COLOSSIANS 1 : 2.)[4]

This is not just a pretty little theory. Christadelphians really do think of one another as brothers and sisters, and they take a close and practical interest in one another's welfare. They are usually on first-name terms, but when they are not they address each other as Brother X or Sister Y – never as Mr., Mrs., or Miss.

This brothering and sistering is the only touch of quaintness that the newcomer to a Christadelphian meeting is likely to encounter. We dress normally, we speak normal (but clean) English, we behave like normal, decent people. Our first-century religion is fully adapted to its twentieth-century environment.

Self Government

The early church had no paid clergy, and no national or international headquarters. The first-century Christians got along quite well without those things, and so do the Christadelphians today.

Each Christadelphian meeting is self-governing, being responsible only to its own members and to Christ, its unseen leader. Its ministers are all laymen serving the church in their spare time; they would no more think of accepting payment than would the fishermen of Galilee who formed Christ's first disciples. Their qualifications for the work are a sound knowledge of the Bible and a sound manner of life.

There are virtually no rules governing membership, except those laid down by the Bible itself. Should anyone openly rebel against Christ's teaching – an unrepentant adulterer, for instance – they are not allowed to remain in fellowship.

But in general the Christadelphian does not expect his church to discipline him. He reckons, with God's help, to discipline himself.

If he is in earnest about his religion he sets himself very high ideals, just as men did in the first-century church. He doesn't always manage to maintain his high standards, but at least he keeps on trying.

Let me make it absolutely clear that what follows is not a description of a typical Christadelphian, nor even of a particularly fine one. It is a picture of the target we are always aiming at, but which none of us ever quite reaches.

High Ideals

Christ had no time for immorality, and neither has any Bible-based church. Chastity, honesty and truthfulness are all musts for the genuine Christian.

At the same time, Christ hates self-righteousness, hard-heartedness and unkindness. He condemned the smug bunch of Pharisees who were looking down their noses at an adulterous woman – and then he rebuked the woman, 'Go, and do not sin again.' (JOHN 8 : 11.)

The lesson of this story is clear. Christ hates both sorts of sin: the hidden sins of the heart, like the hypocrisy of the Pharisees, and the more obvious sins, like the adultery of the woman.

So we must constantly fight against 'internal' sins, like pride, and covetousness, and unclean thoughts; but we must fight equally hard against the 'external' sins, like cheating the income tax man, gluttony, and lying our way out of a scrape.

But this is only the negative side of Christian behaviour – the 'thou shalt nots'. Equally important, maybe even more important, are the positive traits listed in GALATIANS 5 : 22,23.

'The fruit of the Spirit is love, joy, peace, patience, kindness, goodness, faithfulness, gentleness, self-control.'

Let's look at those pieces of fruit one by one, and see what they really mean in practice.

Fruit of the Spirit

Love. The word Paul used means, 'Christlike love.' Not just natural affection, but the outgoing, genuine concern for other men and women that puts them first and me last.

Joy. Am I a wet blanket, a Dismal Willie of a Christian? Or has Christ brought joy into my life, the deep, abiding happiness that rubs off me on to others and enriches their lives too?

Peace. There is no room for quarrelling in Christ's family. Christ died in agony to give us peace with God. We must not spoil that heavenly peace by earthly bickering.

Patience. Paul's word really meant tenacity, the ability to hang on however rough the ride becomes. Am I a sticker? Or do I give in far too easily, when sacrifice is called for?

Kindness. Time after time when Jesus saw people in trouble he was 'moved with compassion', and came to the rescue. Am I like that? Or do I pass by on the other side of the road?

Goodness. The very word has an old-fashioned ring about it. Goodness – decency, if you like – is in short supply nowadays. No Christian can afford to be without it.

Faithfulness. There is not much of this about nowadays, either. People say, 'You can't rely upon anybody.' Do they say that of me, too? They won't, if I develop faithfulness.

Gentleness. Some of the qualities listed above call for a tough streak. It is difficult to be a Christian without it. But the true Christian will only get really tough with himself. Gentleness is the face he will turn towards his fellow men.

Self-control. Do I run my life as if pleasure and self fulfilment were the only things that mattered? Or do I keep self on a chain, like the dangerous animal it is? Do I give God the first call on my energy, my time, my abilities and my money? Because this is the way of real discipleship. Jesus said:

'Do not start worrying: "Where will my food come from? or my drink? or my clothes?" (These are the things the heathen are always after.) Your Father in heaven knows that you need all these things. Instead, *give first place to his Kingdom and to what he requires,* and he will provide you with all these other things.' (MATTHEW 6: 31–33, TEV.)

If you feel you could never begin to rise to such high ideals, remember one thing. Paul called these things 'the fruit of the Spirit', for a very good reason.

Despite all the marvels of modern science, man still does not know how to manufacture an orange. Yet trees produce fruit easily, through the strange powers locked up within their cells. Similarly, God's Spirit is able to produce 'fruit' in those who let that Spirit work in their lives. The Spirit of God is another name for the Power of God,[5] and that almighty power can work wonders in helping you to develop a Christlike character.

Indeed, God has the power to perform miracles. He will work a miracle within you – if you let Him.

10

CAN WE AFFORD IT?

Sensible people always think carefully before they buy something. A new car, for instance.

What is the basic price? How much a week will that work out at? Then what about the running costs – tax, insurance, garage rent, petrol, oil, tyres, servicing, spares, and so on? In short, how much is it going to cost me overall? Can I really afford it? Will the benefit of having it make the expenses worthwhile?

That is an example of a well-known situation, where someone works out the cost of doing something. But there are a lot of other situations, much less pleasant, when you have to work out a different sort of cost – the cost of *not* doing something. This one, for example.

It is Saturday morning and you are just setting out on holiday in your new car. To your horror a knock starts up in the engine. What's to be done?

The temptation is to ignore it, to press on and hope the knock will go away. But that would be very risky. You might break down on some lonely mountain road when all the garages in the district are shut for the weekend, and find yourself stranded until Monday. That would be a fine start to your holiday!

Reluctantly, you face the fact that you're up against it. There is only one safe way to act. You postpone your departure by a few hours and take the car to your local dealer for attention.

In this second situation you don't really have much choice. In such circumstances you weigh up the cost of doing nothing – and, inevitably, you conclude that you simply must take action to avoid unpleasant consequences.

The Lord Jesus Christ once told a couple of parables outlining these two types of situation.[1]

He began by talking of a man who wanted to build a tower. Of course the man prices the whole job before he starts; he would cut a sorry figure if he built the bottom half and then ran out of money.

Becoming a Christian is like that, warned Jesus. Don't rush into it without stopping to think; weigh up the cost before you start. It is a big thing to follow the Son of God: you had better not begin if it is going to be too much for you.

Perhaps Jesus saw some of his listeners shaking their heads at that point. So he went on with his second parable, about a man who was forced to weigh up the cost of doing nothing.

This man was a king. Not much of a king, apparently, because his army was only ten thousand strong. One day bad news reached him. Another king, with an army of twenty thousand, was on the warpath and heading his way.

It did not take the first king long to assess his position. To do nothing would be disastrous. That would mean invasion, defeat, conquest. No, he could not possibly afford to sit back and hope that his enemy would go away.

Swiftly he took the only practical step open to him: 'I must send an ambassador to negotiate a peace treaty while there is still time!'

And that, according to Jesus, is the sort of plight that all of us are in. We are all on a collision course with the King and Judge of the world, unless we take steps to make peace with Him.

So weigh up the cost of becoming a disciple by all means. But don't stop there. Weigh up also the conse-quences of *not* becoming one, and you will soon realise that there is only one course for sensible men and women to follow.

Time is not on your side, either. Not so long ago people

sneeringly called religion the old folks' game. They had
not long to live; it was natural for the aged to prepare
to meet their God. But young men and women were different; they could afford to wait a while.

Even if that was true then, it is not now. Who can say
how many years our tormented civilisation still has to
live?

We are all like old men and women today

Society could begin to crumble in ruins tomorrow,
bringing death and destruction to young and old alike.

Christ offers us a refuge from the coming storm, giving
us peace of mind and comfort here and now, and the sure
promise of everlasting life in his glorious kingdom in days
to come.

Can you possibly afford to turn him down?

NOTES AND REFERENCES

Chapter 1

1 Debate on the Hydrogen Bomb, 1 March, 1955.
2 *Daily Telegraph*, London, 25 April 1975, p. 5.
3 Ronald Higgins, 'The seventh enemy'. *Observer Magazine*, 23 February 1975, pp. 14–23.
4 H. G. Wells, *Mind at the End of Its Tether* (Heinemann, London, 1945) ch. 1.

Chapter 2

1 Cited by John Wesley White, in *Re-Entry* (Zondervan, Grand Rapids, 1971) ch. 1.
2 I am indebted for this information to my friend Dr. L. A. Eyre of The University of The West Indies, the geographer and historian. He was personally acquainted with the late Mrs. Ella Ray, who recalled seeing President Lincoln at Christadelphian meetings in Washington when she was a girl.
3 John Wesley White, op cit.
4 See, for example, Newton's Exposition of Daniel.
5 Edward Gibbon, *Decline & Fall of the Roman Empire*, vol. 4, ch. 15, 'The progress of the Christian religion – sentiments, manners, numbers and conditions of the primitive Christians.'
6 As Paul indicated in Colossians 1 : 23, this had a small-scale fulfilment within the next forty years or so, when the gospel was preached throughout the 'world' that the Jews knew. This Jewish 'world' came crashing to its end, when the Romans destroyed Jerusalem. But the main fulfilment has had to await our own day.
7 The Lord's thoughts in this passage are complex. The introduction to the passage seems to link it to the troubles of the first century, but its conclusion clearly relates to our twen-

tieth-century problems. It probably means that Daniel's prophecy had a partial fulfilment in the first century, but will not have its complete fulfilment until the time of the Second Coming.

Chapter 3

1, 2 Students of the Old Testament will recognise these expressions, which are used by the prophets as parable-language to indicate the collapse of governments. See Isaiah 13 : 5–13, for example.

Chapter 4

1 All the people mentioned by name in this book are real, and the stories recounted are true, but the names have been changed (except the names of celebrities.)

2 I have dealt with this in detail in *GOD'S TRUTH – A scientist shows why it makes sense to believe the Bible*. (Marshall, Morgan & Scott, London, 1973.)

3 C. S. Lewis, in his masterly work, to which this chapter is very much indebted, 'Right and wrong as a clue to the meaning of the universe.' (From *Mere Christianity*, Geoffrey Bles, London, 1952.)

4 This also is dealt with in *GOD'S TRUTH*. (See 2, above.)

Chapter 6

1 See, for example, Hebrews 9 : 15 and 1 Corinthians 11 : 25.

2 **A table of daily Bible readings for beginners,** *Getting to Know the Bible,* **will help you here. Obtainable free on request from the publishers of this book.**

Chapter 7

1 'Gehenna fire' (hell fire) is mentioned only in the New Testament. In the Old Testament the word 'hell' is never connected with fire. It is found in the King James Version of the Old Testament, where it is the translation of a Hebrew word, *Sheol*, which is actually a poetical name for the grave. Modern translators usually leave the word untranslated (as *Sheol*) or translate it, 'the grave'. See, for example, Isaiah 14 : 15–20. The Greek word for *Sheol* is *Hades*, which occurs in a few places in the New Testament. It is used, for ex-

ample, of the grave that Jesus was buried in; see Acts
2 : 25–31.

2 There are one or two Bible passages where the word 'soul' at
first sight appears to refer to an immortal spirit. But closer
examination soon reveals that this is not really what is
meant, and that these isolated passages do not disagree with
the other 500 or so passages where 'soul' is always related to
our present mortal existence.

3 Strictly speaking the International Distress Signal, SOS, does
not stand for anything – it just happens to be a very distinc-
tive pattern of dots and dashes in Morse. But the popular
interpretation, 'Save our souls', illustrates the real meaning
of the word *soul*.

Chapter 8

1 For a detailed explanation see my pamphlet, *The Problem
of Suffering*, obtainable from the publishers of this book.

2 From the Appendix of his *Historical Essays and Studies*.

3 So 1 Corinthians 15 : 28 indicates.

Chapter 9

1 Bertrand Russell, *Power* (George Allen & Unwin, London,
1938) ch. 7.

2 G. C. Field, *Pacifism and Conscientious Objection* (University Press, Cambridge, 1945) ch. 3, p. 78.

3 This can be inferred from several New Testament passages,
notably Acts 20 : 7 and 1 Corinthians 16 : 2.

4 Greek, *Christō adelphoi*.

5 To see that this is so, compare the promise of Luke 24 : 49 –
'power from on high' – with its restatement in Acts 1 : 8 –
'power when the Holy Spirit has come upon you'. Also, see
Luke 1 : 35, where 'the Holy Spirit' is paralleled with 'the
power of the Most High'.

Chapter 10

1 Luke 14 : 27–33.

PUBLISHERS' NOTE

Having read the book you will no doubt wish to pursue your interest by making contact with Christadelphians or taking advantage of the offer of a Bible reading plan on page 94.

You might also like to contact the Christadelphian meeting nearest to your home. In many areas you will find the address amongst the Church notices of a local newspaper. In some places you will find the name 'Christadelphian' listed in the telephone directory.

In whatever part of the world you live we can put you in touch with members of the Christadelphian community, or send you further reading matter, just as you wish.

Write to us at:

CHRISTADELPHIANS WORLDWIDE
DEPT. 153B
3 REGENT STREET
BIRMINGHAM B1 3HG, ENGLAND